THE LIGHT

To 'W.E.' whose constancy in wisdom and loving kindness has brought this book into being.

THE LIGHT
IN BRITAIN

GRACE AND IVAN COOKE

THE WHITE EAGLE PUBLISHING TRUST
NEW LANDS · LISS · HAMPSHIRE

First published 1971
Sixth impression 1995

ISBN *0-85487-056-3*

Printed in Great Britain
at the University Press, Cambridge

FOREWORD

OUR purpose in this book is to reveal something of the pure and holy light which ancient Brotherhoods in Britain have left as our heritage and for our blessing—a light which (as in the age-old legend of King Arthur and his knights) lies dormant, only waiting to break forth to inspire and lead the people to victory over the darkness of materialism.

CONTENTS

	FOREWORD	V
	LIST OF ILLUSTRATIONS	viii
	PREFACE TO THE 1983 EDITION	ix
	ACKNOWLEDGMENTS	x
	INTRODUCTION	1
I	*Together we set off*	3
II	*Trackway into the Magical Land*	8
III	*When the Dragon was Slain on Dragon Hill*	16
IV	*The Silversmith of Souls*	26
V	*The King's Men*	36
VI	*We visit the Trodden-under-foot Cathedral*	43
VII	*When the Angel of the Sun came over Stonehenge*	54
VIII	*When the Serpent rose Heavenward*	69
IX	*Maiden of the High Hills*	83
X	*Religion Pure and Undefiled*	92
XI	*Britain Arise!*	101
	Epilogue	106
	APPENDIX	109

LIST OF ILLUSTRATIONS

1	*Silbury Hill long ago* (artist's impression)	7
2	*The Great Ridgeway* (artist's impression)	10
3	*The Berkshire Ridgeway today*	13
4	*Dragon Hill* (artist's impression)	18
5	*Dragon Hill from Uffington Castle*	22
6	*An aerial view of the 'dragon'*	22
7	*Wayland's Smithy* (artist's impression)	28
8	*The entrance to the Smithy*	31
9	*The Rollright Stones*	40
10	*A reconstruction of the temple of Avebury*	46
11	*Avebury from the air*	49
12	*Stonehenge today*	57
13	*A map of Stonehenge*	63
14	*St. David's Head*	72
15	*Maiden Castle*	89

This book was first published in 1971 and its republication is in response to the continuing demand for it. Considerable work has been done in archaeology and cosmology since it was conceived but it is felt that the importance of the book lies in the purity of the vision that it transmits. We have left unaltered reference to scientific theories which are no longer widely held because we feel that the insights the authors give even in discussing these theories are themselves valuable.

ACKNOWLEDGMENTS

Acknowledgments are due to Messrs. Batsford for permission to quote from *The English Downland* by Hugh Massingham; to Messrs. Methuen for the quotation from *The Green Roads of England* by R. Hippisley Cox; and to Messrs. Daniel for the quotation from *The Teachings of the Essenes from Enoch to the Dead Sea Scrolls* by Edmond Bordeaux Szekely.

Of the illustrations, numbers 1, 2, 4 and 7 are reproduced from paintings by Ivan Cooke; numbers 3, 5 and 8 from photographs by Colum and Jeremy Hayward; and the aerial photographs, numbers 6, 9, 11, 12, 14 and 15, are by Aerofilms Ltd. The reconstruction of Avebury, number 10, is by Alan Sorrell, and reproduced by kind permission of the Ministry of Public Building and Works. The map of Stonehenge, number 13, is reproduced from the Ordnance Survey Map, with the sanction of the Controller of H.M. Stationery Office, Crown Copyright Reserved. The cover illustration is from an original oil painting by Ivan Cooke.

INTRODUCTION

My wife's powers of seership first manifested during her childhood, and her life since has been largely dedicated to their development and establishment—to their testing and proving. Her name, Grace Cooke, will be familiar to a wide circle, through the many books of the White Eagle Publishing Trust. In particular, another book of hers, *The Illumined Ones*, should be recognised as this book's forerunner, in that it also delves into a period perhaps ten, twenty thousand years ago, and recounts her memory of a life she herself lived as a Mayan girl. This story is told with simplicity and charm, but with an admixture of the wise and deep philosophy taught and practised by the ancient Mayas, who at that period were a simple, happy race and brotherly in all their ways. The wise and great Hah-wah-tah of those days, whom she describes as her father, is that same White Eagle who has been her companion and spiritual teacher throughout her present life and through many incarnations, and whose wisdom illumines this present book. The name itself is symbolic of a spiritual teacher, a messenger.

The story in *The Illumined Ones* 'keys in,' as it were, with *The Light in Britain* in another way also, because the ancients, contrary to general belief, mingled freely, voyaged freely across the oceans, and were citizens not only of their country but of their world, and may well have touched the shores of Britain. So it is to the very ancient British people, perhaps of an earlier humanity and living in a wiser, kindlier, more

I

sensible and brotherly world, that this our book would seek to introduce its readers. It is the story of a light dwelling in the heart of Britain and her people.

Also what my wife and I want very much to feel is that our reader is ready to share in this quest with us; ready in imagination to climb the downlands, to feel their wholesomeness and power, to respond to their spirit and message. We want to pursue this quest together. So whenever in future the pronoun 'we' occurs it is meant to include our reader—even if you feel distrustful at first about the revelations of seership. We shall grow closer during our journey, closer than you might think; and who knows—might presently climb to heights most blest up on our chalk downs, and reach and find an aloneness set high between heaven and earth, where larks sing and sweet grasses and herbs scent the pure winds. Here shall we find the secret of Britain's lost heritage waiting for us to rediscover, waiting to reveal itself.

I

TOGETHER WE SET OFF

THIS is a story of adventure; and of an investigation by somewhat unorthodox methods into the ancient heritage of this mystic Isle of Britain.

One bright summer day in early June 1966, my husband, myself and Jenny, our granddaughter, set off in happy anticipation to explore the beauties of some of the English chalk downland, in high hopes that we should learn something more concerning the kind of life lived by the ancient Britons.

Many years before I had been deeply impressed by an article in one of the daily papers describing excavations and discoveries then being made at Avebury in Wiltshire, of what was thought to be a sun temple of considerable antiquity. The writer of the article said that when the excavations and restorations were complete, and all the huge stones re-erected, the ancient temple would prove to be grander and more impressive than any known Egyptian temple. A diagram showed the plan of these ancient stones as they might look when re-erected in their original positions.

Excited by what I read then, my family and I had set off to explore Avebury. It proved to be a medley of immense monoliths scattered over many acres of the countryside, some of the stones actually standing in the gardens of the cottages of Avebury. About a mile distant from the village, close to the Bath Road, stood a strange artificial hill known as Silbury Hill. We now know that this inexplicable hill, with a base covering several acres, and rising from a flat meadow, has defeated all the archaeological experts right up to the present day in their effort to find any explanation for its existence. Then, it was all strange to us, and we knew nothing of its fame.

I felt a magnetic attraction towards this hill; it was drawing me and I wanted to climb to the top and hastened to do so. Once up there, a magnificent view of the surrounding country-side opened out, but most striking to me was a bird's-eye view of the lines of stones of Avebury, which looked as though they had first been laid out in the form of a curving serpent. From above it was apparent that many of the larger stones were missing, but sufficient of the smaller monoliths remained to give me the impression that this may have been the site of some so-called serpent-worship of prehistoric time, about which I had once read. We felt a power so strong that we had to linger at the top. For some reason, in spite of the cold March day, it no longer felt cold or blustery.

Gradually my etheric vision awakened and I saw that the area about the hill was filled with nature spirits of all kinds, and I realised that I was watching a ceremony of the 'rogation' or the 'blessing of the seeds' taking place, which seemed to call forth a great deal of sound and movement on the etheric plane. I could also see many women and children at the foot of the hill, busily sowing the seeds. Then I felt a tremendous heat all around me on the hilltop and saw with amazement an immense altar upon which a great flame arose—it burnt quite unlike any ordinary fire, for it seemed to need no replenish-ment; and I felt that it had been burning there in the etheric world for unmeasured time. Great beings who seemed to be the high priests were serving at this altar.

Strangely enough, the impression given to me was that some of these people on the hill were (or had once been) Indians with feathered head-dresses,* and that others were of the Egyptian race. They in turn were controlling and directing an army of agricultural workers on the plains below, by what appeared to me to be remote, telepathic or even automatic control. Also I saw many etheric people assisting the men and women below, while the priests standing by the altar were directing on to the earth streams of white light, nourishment drawn from the ether for dressing the newly sown land.

While this ceremony was in progress, there appeared those whom I felt to be planetary visitors coming from outer space to share in what was really a festival in celebration of the vernal equinox. Normally we should have been shivering by now on any hilltop on such a bitterly cold day; but personally I felt that I was bathed in warmth as though the sun were blazing down on me.

This vision on Silbury Hill stirred other memories deep in my soul, memories which had hardly taken form but which made me resolve that later on, when the threat of war had ceased, and we could move freely and perhaps spend more time in quiet contemplation, we would re-visit this strangely attractive spot.

*   *   *

Thus on a lovely June day in 1966 we again set forth, not

---

* Some years after this unforgettable experience, my memory was once again stirred, and I was able to look back into my own past and see myself as a South American Indian girl. I am convinced that there is a link between what I saw on Silbury, and the very ancient Mayan civilisation in which I once lived. I am sure that many of the etheric beings and spirits that I saw had once been American Indians. Their dress and their mode of perambulation around the hill, their method of directing the white rays across the fields and plains were similar to the dress worn and ceremonies practised by the Indians who lived in the foothills of the Andes so many, many years ago.

I have been led increasingly to believe that this ceremony so clearly shown to me in the precincts of the ancient serpent-worship temple near Avebury, was originally introduced into Britain by those South American Indians who had much knowledge of etheric life.

5

only to investigate the mysteries of Avebury, but to visit other prehistoric sites which from my inner knowledge I now believed to be connected with an ancient brotherhood of sainted people, members of a race which once lived in Britain.

We planned to stay in Marlborough, a favourite centre from which to visit the famous White Horse of Uffington on the Berkshire Downs; and then go on to Wayland's Smithy, where, according to our guide-book, we should find a dolmen or burial-chamber. From here we would travel on to Avebury, and later to the Rollright Stones in the Cotswolds.

We spent some time in meditation at each of these ancient centres, in the course of which I was taken back in memory, in awareness, to religious rituals enacted at these places in ages long past; and as I described these etheric scenes, Jenny, our granddaughter, recorded it in shorthand.

Here I must explain that all physical form has its etheric counterpart, and that all human life and thought impresses itself on the 'ether' or the etheric emanation from the physical life of our earth. The life a man leads leaves an impression on the ether around him. Even the commonplace, the ordinary life, leaves such an impression—if any life is ever ordinary. But where some wise and kind man has lived and worked, the impression remains for ever. Thus the lives of all the ancient peoples who once walked the earth are indelibly impressed upon the ether in records which can be tapped and brought to life by the trained clairvoyant.

These were the records I was reading when we sat in meditation at these ancient centres, and I recounted what I saw for Jenny to record.

Now let my husband take over the story.

1   *Silbury Hill long ago* (artist's impression)

II

TRACKWAY INTO THE MAGICAL LAND

> Those who desire to receive accurately from the higher
> worlds must learn to discipline their minds, to preserve
> tranquillity and quietude of the soul . . . must learn to move
> harmoniously, quietly, obediently, through life. Then only
> will they reflect truth, think and speak truth, and live truth.
>
> W.E.

IN fancy we have climbed high and are now walking along the
Great Ridgeway, one of the oldest roads in our land. We do
not know how many generations of men have trodden this
ancient trackway, and died in this Britain of ours. What we
call 'ancient' history only reaches back a few thousand years
and is based on findings of the bones of men, their bits of pottery and domestic tools, and the discovery of even earlier
relics such as the fossilised bones of semi-tropical animals. We
know from these that Britain once possessed a warmer and
more genial climate, but concerning the men and women of
long-ago we know nothing except certain myths or folk-tales
that have come down to us. Someone once said that a myth is
fossilised history—a folk-tale which has become embedded in
the race and has come down perhaps through countless generations to acquire the semblance of a fairy-tale, a fantasy; but a
fantasy which embodies deep and ancient truths.

A trackway starts as far north as the Wash and as the
Icknield Way traverses the great backbone of the Chilterns,
and so to the Berkshire Downs where an ancient track links
it with that Great Ridgeway which follows the crest of the
Berkshire and Marlborough Downs from Streatley to Avebury,

skirts Salisbury Plain, with arms reaching out to touch Stonehenge and many another centre of ancient worship; and then onward, ever winding up and down to finish in Devonshire.

High above the swamps and forests which, in days far gone, formed the greater part of Britain, this noble trackway strode across the hills, while many generations of men, our own spiritual ancestors, walked along it, spent their whole being amid those hills, and loving them also loved each other. They intermarried and brought forth children; and in all their aspirations, hopes and fears which comprise human life, the trackway shared. And because it has known these deep human feelings, they are implanted in its substance, have become part of its very being, giving it atmosphere; so that whoever walks the trackway and breathes its atmosphere will know that these thoughts and feelings of long ago are as real as ours today, once one can respond to them.

Of this trackway H. J. Massingham wrote in *The English Downland*: '. . . the majesty of the great trackway is the threefold one of site, of conception and of time . . . the Ridgeway travelling the Berkshire Downs is the greatest, the lengthiest, and the noblest in appearance of all the prehistoric roads.

'. . . It looks its part. In places twenty and often forty yards and more in width, and bounded, though not all the way, by low tangled banks, by thorn, maple, spindle, black bryony and travellers joy, spaced out at irregular intervals, or by short and occasional rows of beeches, it flows westwards in a series of mighty undulations towards Avebury, the London of the megalith builders. . . . But it is unlike any of the Roman roads in Berkshire . . . because it is always bending from the straight to circumvent the trouble the Romans gave themselves by pushing their will against every natural resistance. This double motion, absent from the Roman road, adds

variety to its dignity, and seems to endow it with every grace in fluctuation of surface which the downs possess. The old road is theirs, its movement is of their rhythm, its course a sensitive reaction to their forms. . . . The Great Ridgeway's natural affinity is more with the sky above it than with the valley from which its humbler consort is barely raised. The skyey influence is in constant play with the surface of the downs, directly by the cloud-shadows that stalk over it, and indirectly by the elevated plateau communicating the heavenly quality of spaciousness. It is an enlargement shared by the road in its breadth and easy movement and gestures of rise and fall, and by the human spirit that follows its trail. That spirit is assured of a silence deepened rather than broken by the winds and the purified voices of the skylarks, whose airy chain of syllables travels twice as far as in the plain.

'Encountering but one house, where the Wantage–Hungerford road severs the Green Way, the walker will be at home in a solitude that is never estranging, because the massiveness of curve and fold is accompanied by a gentleness in their structure whose meaning is welcome. Here are no crags to dwarf nor precipices to repulse the man among them, and the great road, man-made and at one with the downs, is the intermediary between human feeling and the high places its early deities once walked.'

A noble description of a noble road! Surely there must be few who can walk this great trackway untouched, unfeeling, without opening themselves to welcome its spirit and abiding power. This is a magical trackway. In Berkshire, high over the

2 *The Great Ridgeway, which stretched half way across England in ancient times. In the valley to the left is the edge of the vast swampland which is now the Thames Valley* (artist's impression)

little Dragon Hill at Uffington, one encounters strong and righteous magic; one can stand here where the steep hill falls directly away to the great 'horse' long ago carved in the hill-side chalk (which some say, and very reasonably, is no horse at all but represents a flying dragon) and look across this highly stylised beast down to the valley, to where beyond the village of Uffington, the land drops into that vast decline which is the Thames Valley. And as we stand and gaze we can feel not only the power of the ancient life bequeathed the memories that now stir within us, but also the possibility that we ourselves in some incarnation long ago once trod this 'green road' and standing on this high place, ourselves looked down.

Below White Horse Hill, and looking towards Uffington, is a smallish flat-topped hill, its base covering about an acre, quite obviously man-made, by men carrying earth up to its crown—how many generations ago no one knows. If you will climb and walk across that hilltop you wonder why, although the soil seems fertile enough, there is a barren area where nothing will grow. No kind of turf will you find, nor yet flowers. Legend has it that here on this flat-topped hill our own St. George fought long and desperately with the dragon and slew it, and that its blood, gushing forth, flooded that flat top, since when nothing green has ever grown there.

Our folk stories, and indeed myths from all over the world, are charged with tales of fearful dragons, all representing evil in personified form, all breathing fire and destruction, all eager to kill innocence, integrity, fidelity and good intent.

So in imagination we now stand and gaze, and ponder on the origin and meaning of these stories. We look back along the trackway, and perhaps there comes over us a feeling as of

3   *The Berkshire Ridgeway today: looking East to Uffington Castle*

living long ago when the climate was warmer and more sensitive; when plants and fruits and crops flourished on these high downs. And then as we again look across the great valley of the Thames, behold, all is changed! Gone is Uffington village, gone are the orderly fields, the nestling woodlands, the gentle tree-lined countryside; and now before us, spread right across the valley we see only pools of water and the slush of great swamps matted together, all full of shadow and threat of darkness, where one could only walk or creep through tunnelled ways, ever shaded from the sky, giving no vista of the hills. Our thoughts come back for a moment to the present, and we wonder whether our own tunnelled roads, and our (so to speak) tunnelled lives spent in cities, are in some way a reflection of matted swamp lands, and whether we have got into the habit, as our ancestors did, of choosing shaded ways in which to hide and live? Do we now somehow fear the vast spaces of the downs? Can this be true?

Well, we have come to a place where mighty happenings have been wrought, and soon we are going to employ the power of clear-vision, of clear-seeing, that aspect of clear-seeing which is the power to investigate ancient truths of long ago, to re-establish them in the thought and mind, and possibly in the very being of man; so that he sees whence he came, and better, knows why he is here, and gets more than a glimpse, a hope—gets a firm belief as to whither he will go when his days in the flesh are ended. In short, this is a clear-seeing which can reveal to a man a world which although seeming disorderly is in fact ordered and planned, with man's destiny clear before him, and the reason of his being and the way he should try to live.

In this first message statements will be made about the life of man in the long ago when he lived to a far greater age, and during his span—say of six score years—acquired greater vision of the truth, greater wisdom, greater measure of health, and strength, greater capacity to deal with the world about him than we who live only for half his period, never reaching to our full span of life or vigour, either mental or physical.

These are some of the things we shall have to take in our stride for the moment. Each and all will come to be explained, to be given credence, become open to belief, although not all at once. For the moment certain things will have to be taken on trust, and the reader will help himself by remaining open and receptive to new and perhaps strange ideas.

III

WHEN THE DRAGON WAS SLAIN
ON DRAGON HILL

There are centres in this mystic Isle of Britain where a
great, a perfect light has been accumulating for centuries—
centres where long ago sincere and holy brethren met to
practise the mysteries. Upon tnem a blazing golden light
poured down, and through them it impregnated the very
earth itself . . .   W.E.

THE three of us, my wife, Jenny and myself are seated high on
the Berkshire Downs hard by Uffington Castle, a great
circular earthwork rising to nearly one thousand feet, flanked
by numerous barrows where the revered dead have been
interred. We have edged away from the crowd, for this is a
popular spot, and being away from the world seem raised high
above it—literally so, for the world lies flattened at our feet.
Behind us Uffington Castle rises high against the skyline, and
behind it again runs the great trackway, smooth and green,
carpeted, as it has been through the centuries, by fine well-
trodden turf. Just below can be seen the White Horse or
Dragon, the oldest known figure ever carved in the chalk in
Britain. It is said to be two thousand years old at least, and has
been kept clear throughout the centuries.

The countrymen used to sing:

> The Owld White Horse wants zettin' to rights,
> And the Squire has promised good cheer,
> Zo we'll gi'us a scrape to kip un in shape,
> And a'll last for many a year.

16

All is very quiet. Jenny is waiting with a pencil and note-book ready, and the person most necessary is quietly opening the deeper levels within herself. She now responds to the atmosphere, to the all-pervading influence, to the surrounding ether and its record of the past ages. She sees what once happened as pictures, but 'alive' pictures; that is to say, she is projected into the past so that it is real to her and she is living in it.

It must be noted that not only in this, but in all the visionary experiences that follow, she will touch on many different periods and strata of human experience. Some of the visions go back to lives lived in an inconceivably distant past, and others are comparatively closer in time. In some, several different periods kaleidoscope. It will be noted also what a range of speculation and even revelation is opened up. Indeed, is not this place sufficient to inspire such a message, with the larks singing high above the chalk hills, and the scent of wild thyme upon the air?

THE WHITE HORSE AND DRAGON HILL

White Horse Hill: five miles west of Wantage. The sketchy figure of a horse (375 ft. long) cut in the turf on the hillside is of unknown origin, but thought to be of great antiquity, probably late Iron Age. The hollow on the west face of the hill is known as the 'manger' slightly to the north of which is a detached knoll called Dragon Hill, where, according to local tradition, St. George slew the dragon.

The message begins:

'The dragon symbolises darkness and evil, conquered by the power of the light. The legend of St. George and the dragon tells the same story. St. George symbolises the light (or Christ in man) and all that is good, the dragon all that is evil. There

17

was a concentration of the light here to dispel the darkness. But first there was a terrific battle on the etheric plane between the forces of good and evil. This was an Atlantean colony. The dark priests from Atlantis gained knowledge of destructive power which could have destroyed the earth. There was a concentration of the dark power set up here which had to be overcome by the light.

'I can now see a great open-air temple there below. I can see a procession of people with torches, proceeding round and round, enacting a ceremony to invoke the light to penetrate the darkness centred on Dragon's Hill. A great battle took place between these dark forces and the light, a battle which manifested right through on to the physical plane, where there was bloodshed and carnage. The people of the light came from far to bring the light to the young souls, who would have none of it. Then followed the battle. I feel that all around this hill was water and marshland where swamp people lived, while the people of the light lived on the surrounding hills high above the darkness. They fought and won the battle with darkness and ignorance, the dragon was slain, and Dragon Hill purified by their invocation of the light.

'On these hills an observatory* was built, from which the people of the light watched the heavens. They were not ignorant, but very knowledgeable, particularly about the etheric worlds. They were the true Britons; they were not called Britons then, but were known by another name.

'I can now see Dragon Hill ablaze with gold; it has become

* See Appendix, p. 108.

4   *A torchlight procession round Dragon Hill at dawn, in ancient times. Above Dragon Hill is the image of the dragon cut into the chalk hillside, the remains of which are known today as the Uffington 'Horse' (artist's impression)*

a hill of gold. This place has to do with the serpent. I can see the people processing in the form of a serpent. I can hear the rhythmic tramp, tramp, tramp and music working up to a crescendo as the people perambulate round the hill, singing and bearing blazing torches—this was an age-old magical rite, a celebration of the triumph of the light over the dragon of evil, which arises out of ignorance. The white horse on the hill is really the symbol of the dragon—commemorating this battle between the forces of light and darkness.'

Sometime after this experience above Dragon Hill, I turned up yet another description, this time of my wife's first visit, in October 1949. It is interesting to see how far the two messages corroborate one another. The 1949 message reads:

'We climbed up past Dragon Hill, past the shape of the horse or dragon cut into the side of White Horse Hill, to the castle above, and stood facing the great valley of the Thames with its horizon of hills. The sun was a deep gold as it set in a cloudless sky, casting a soft amethyst light over the hills and valleys, which in the distance changed to the soft blue that to me symbolises the Great Mother Spirit.

'It was a wonderful scene even on the physical plane. But as I went into meditation my inner vision slowly opened and I saw a great assembly of simply-clad people filling the amphitheatre or 'manger' below Dragon Hill, and heard the sound of trumpets, summoning the people to take part in some grand ceremony of sun worship. I saw then that twelve high priests were conducting the ritual now taking place on Dragon Hill, and they appeared to be summoning the great angels of the White Light. For in the white ether which was now rising from above the altar (they were using the hill as an altar) I saw especially angels which I thought were from other planets; and around the hill itself there seemed to be a host of lesser nature spirits, sylphs and salamanders, gnomes and other fairy forms. They too, with the people, seemed to move round the base of the hill, encircling it many times. While they did so I saw an ever-rising spiral of golden light. Presently the ritual rose to a kind of crescendo called forth by the chanting people; they seemed to glow with light, while the radiation appeared as a fountain of light, rising and spreading out over the surrounding countryside so that a golden radiance fell on the earth.

'I felt that a great being was enveloped within this light and thought it might be the Christ-form.* The form gradually became more definite; and then I saw another being appear who seemed like a king, wearing a crown of gold and robed in light, with the points of that crown emitting rays of great brilliance.

'I thought then about King Ar-Thor, the ancient mythical Hyperborian king, and felt that it must be he who had come to bring blessing to his people; and that the whole ceremony had symbolised a form of crucifixion, showing the people how to bring about the overcoming of man's fleshly or material self —the slaying of the dragon of evil within themselves and the subsequent resurrection of the eternal spirit of Christ* ever indwelling in man's heart; all those present were called upon to assist in this divine ascension.'

The foregoing message tells us that the 'dragon' symbolised the powers of darkness or evil in this ancient land, and as shelter and saviour against these attacking powers came the great being called by many names but symbolising always the inmost spirit of man, his innate divinity, his power of self-redemption and sacrifice, symbolising also the inmost spirit of the nation.

* See Appendix, p. 109.

It will be seen that in the first vision this being, this great 'knight of the spirit' is linked with the personality of St. George, and in the second (but earlier one) he is called Ar-Thor. The reference is not presumably to the historical Arthur who led Britain against the Saxon invader, nor is it only to the King Arthur who, with his knights of the Round Table, has come down to us in legend and folk-tale, for the legend itself comes down from a far more ancient past, from that being, Ar-Thor, who, mystically, is the very spirit of Britain, who guides her destiny and will lead her to victory over the powers of evil.

He is called in the vision a 'Hyperborian' king; this brings home a belief set forth by occult tradition, to the effect that there once existed a continent of this name situated to the north of Britain (Hyperborea—literally: the land above the north,) which eventually sank beneath the sea. Tradition says that Hyperborea was inhabited by a race of initiates or wise men. This would account, perhaps, for the many messages which affirm contact or communion with these same wise men in Britain.

Our teacher, White Eagle, has this to say:

THE GOD-MEN OF HYPERBOREA

'In the beginning, the earth was peopled by perfect sons of God who came in all their glory as guardians of a young race on a young planet. These god-men, great and wise brothers, brought the knowledge of the power of the spiritual sun or Christ to the earth. They came first to the land of Hyperborea whose very stones became impregnated with the light they

5   *Dragon Hill today, photographed from Uffington Castle*
6   *An aerial view of the 'dragon' (Aerofilms Ltd.)*

brought to earth. In the course of time these great and wise brothers journeyed across the northern hemisphere taking with them the truth of the light of the sun. Knowledge of sun worship, of the power of the light, swept across the world from that original northern continent of Hyperborea, from the great Sun Brotherhood.

'What you now call Great Britain was once a part of that ancient continent and later of Atlantis. Many of the ancient peoples journeyed here and established here in Britain centres of great spiritual life and power, and this light still lies buried deeply in the very soil of your land. Because of this light, there is in Britain a spiritual power which can and will in future work through all the people of these islands.

'Scientists say that in the ancient days the earth was peopled by primitive creatures, but which of you, even your greatest scientists, can judge of what happened so long ago? The age of the earth and of earth's humanity is beyond man's calculation. We know that it is far, far older than has ever been estimated; and there have been many changes in the earth's surface, and cataclysms which have caused the water to roll where land now exists, and land to be where water is now. There have been civilisations and continents now submerged of which this world knows nothing.* We know that ever since the earth was peopled it has passed through ages of varying consciousness. The human race is not very evolved today but it will become great again when this secret power has been released and the whole vibration of the earth thereby raised. Man himself contains the secret of good or evil. At present the greatest pull would seem to be to evil or to the negative aspect. Man has to make an effort ere the good, the true and the beautiful can dominate his nature. When he can recover from selfishness

* See Appendix, pp. 110, 116.

and overcome this downward pull, then the whole earth will change.'

Could it be that this place where we are now sitting, this Dragon Hill, is one of the ancient sites where the god-men once dwelt and left their light and blessing for future races of men?

IV

THE SILVERSMITH OF SOULS

For ages afterwards the earth-elementals, the nature and air spirits and even the angels themselves have watched over these holy places in Britain, so that even those who are insensitive to spiritual things find themselves drawn thither. They think they go because the place is of historic interest or natural beauty, but we say that within each man is a quality which is attracted by and responds to the influence and the power of these magical places.   W.E.

WE have again climbed up the great trackway, having first stood upon the ramparts of the earthwork fortification called Uffington Castle which crowns the down, marvelling at the patient industry which brought it into being, the infinite labour which went to its construction. And now we set our faces westward to follow the wide Ridgeway where all of ancient Britain once walked. We tread upon their very tracks. Their blood and substance is in our bodies yet, and out on this high place we dimly feel ourselves sharers in their humanity and spirit. The trackway itself brings this feeling to life in us, the atmosphere and scent of the downlands is charged with it. The very ground beneath our feet was once trodden by them; and the turf we tread has grown over and healed many holes and scars which once defaced our trackway, has covered them with its green resilience, and is still gentle to our feet.

We walk westward towards the sun, with all the Thames Valley, where once the swamp-men lived their tunnelled lives, spread out to the north, and before us the rolling downs where our hill-men ancestors walked. What manner of men were

26

these ancestors of ours? We have seen some of their mighty works, which after centuries of weather-attack are still impressive. Most touching of all, we have stood on the barrows where they buried their beloved dead, one would believe with infinite care and reverence, even affording them food and the wherewithal to eat it on their passage to the next world. We know that these peoples were also in touch with Egypt and with Egyptian customs of burial, for beads of Egyptian necklaces have been found within the burial-mounds. Some believe that Egypt itself was once a colony of Atlantis. These hill-men must have faithfully believed that their dead lived on afterwards, and that an unseen but real beneficence ruled their destinies and had power to change the fierce swamp-men if they (the hill-men) played their part.

The few thousand years ago we cite are but a tale of yesterday. What of that sweeter, brighter age of long before, of those more brotherly times when it is said men lived for perhaps double our present life-span, wise and intelligent, and close to their beneficent God?

To find out these things we have become pilgrims, like many others who in days gone by have walked the Great Ridgeway. During our present walk we have traversed perhaps a mile, and now come upon a pile of great stones heaped under a grove of mature beech trees; this is 'Wayland's Smithy' known the world over. Had we ridden here in a mythical long ago, and had our steed cast its shoe and left its rider stranded on these lonely downs, then all that had to be done was for us to tie up that horse hard by the Smithy and steal away (not to witness secret magic), first depositing on the stone a silver coin—of some value, please understand. On our return we would have found our steed magically re-shod, maybe with a silver shoe; although legend is not certain on this point.

At any rate, this is how the centuries-old tale goes, reaching back as far as memory can tell, and embodying a far older myth; for it refers to an ancient mystical teaching about the 'God-shod feet' or the God-guided initiate sometimes symbolised by golden shoes.

In actual fact our little party of three had reached Wayland's Smithy some hours before its visit to Dragon Hill, and was fortunate enough to spend an hour there alone; first walking round the long barrow examining the massive stone beneath which some honoured person had been buried long ago. Everything was favourable. The day was blessed, bright and kindly, and above all no people were around. Having sensed the atmosphere, we settled ourselves comfortably, and the message began to come through.

IMPRESSIONS AT WAYLAND'S SMITHY

According to archaeology: Wayland's Smithy is a Neolithic burial-chamber in a long barrow edged with stones. Beneath the mouth is a smaller long barrow of earlier date, with burials in a wooden chamber.

The message runs: 'I heard music, harmony, singing and chanting whilst we were approaching the entrance. This was once a sun temple and place of initiation. Candidates for initiation came to this spot in the very early days of prehistoric Britain. I contact a ceremony similar to those I have seen connected with the Mayans.* I can see that a special perambulation of the brethren took place here on midsummer day. Then they would stand, waiting for the sun to rise. I can feel a concentration of the rays of the sun and other planets rested on this

* See *The Illumined Ones*.

7 *Wayland's Smithy* (artist's impression)

centre, which became a place of power and worship, bringing about the opening of human consciousness, and unveiling to men knowledge of the real meaning of human life. I feel there were initiations here of young men and women who were ready to follow the path of service. There was once a very wise priest living here. I see that he was a big man with long hair and beard, wearing robes of a material woven in primary colours—yellow, blue and red.

'They studied the heavens here, and I think they even received communications from other planets. Now I see that this priest was nationless, a universal being possessing great wisdom and knowledge, who lived here for many ages.

'All around I can see a camp, not of soldiers, but a travellers' camp, built to accommodate people who had come from far and wide. It looks to me almost like an Indian encampment. The land around is very fertile and has been so for many thousands of years since the time when this land was part of the Atlantean country. For a very ancient Atlantean life once flourished here—this country (Britain) might even have been an island off the coast of Atlantis. The reason why this spot has since been called "Wayland's Smithy" is that many travellers came here seeking for knowledge, direction and guidance from the centre of initiates. They were "re-shod" so that they might "travel" onwards.

'On going even farther back into antiquity, I can see that a great light was concentrated here. I am now in what appears to be a cave. It is a place of worship. I can see a stone altar, embellished by gifts of fruit and sheaves of wheat. These symbols indicate the richness of the harvest, the beauty enriching the lives of the people. I can see that birds and animals of

8   *The entrance to the Smithy*

all kinds have come into this temple to share in the blessing. This is a lovely, lovely place, a place of sunshine, happiness and plenty. All this happened long before history as we know it began.

'Particularly interesting is the jewellery worn by the people. They made such very beautiful jewellery—stones were set in gold and silver, and beautiful beads were used. I also see crowns, head-dresses, bracelets and pottery, where the colours are also bright and impressive, like the colours of flowers. All these people have died and been buried in this lovely country-side.

'I myself feel a definite link with these people, and also a connection with the very ancient Indians of America. They were a gentle, cultured people—it seems as though all this happened before the world sank into its depths of materialism. This spot is sacred because here lie the bones of children and adults, of early kings and queens, of the priests, teachers and even of the initiate head of the people. This has certainly been a centre where men could find initiation into inner truths of life. I feel a connection here with Stonehenge.' (Here the message ends.)

A pilgrim to the Smithy might very well be defined as a 'waylander,' or someone who wends his way across strange lands, and who can easily grow wearied or lost. In other words, his 'horse' (his outer or worldly self) has 'lost a shoe' and become lame. Then at last he comes to that smithy where the kindly smith waits to succour all weary waylanders. But first the waylander must make sacrifice by surrendering something precious to him—say, his silver coin. In other words, some of his worldliness must be foregone, his outer worldly self must humbly sink into abeyance during his initiation of soul and spirit. Even his 'horse' has to become renewed, or 're-shod.' Afterwards he goes forth to seek new tracks across the 'waylands,' not so much across the earthly as across the heavenly places.

Thus it would appear that Wayland's Smithy was an ancient centre of power to which travellers on life's journey came for instruction and initiation into the higher mysteries. Is there a link, perhaps, between the priest figure described, and the Ar-Thor already referred to in the previous chapter?

'All this happened before the race sank into its depths of materialism.' These words would seem to take us back to an even earlier time than the vision of Dragon Hill, before humanity had as yet descended to live altogether a bodily life in a physical environment. This statement denies by implication the accepted theory of evolution, and substitutes instead what the book of Genesis affirms—that man's soul first descended from on high, and that man is fundamentally a spiritual being 'made in God's image.' He lingered for a while on the 'edge' of incarnation, living in a kind of Garden of Eden before descending fully in earthliness, or, as Genesis says, taking on 'coats of skin.'

What White Eagle has to say on this subject also throws light on the battle waged between good and evil already referred to, and the reason for that constant battle.

White Eagle says:

'Scientific thought and teaching of the past century has compelled thinking man to throw aside the old story of the Garden of Eden, yet if you study ancient wisdom you will find much the same legend in the records of many a civilisation which in its turn has risen and passed away. You will say, "But how can we reconcile the myth of the Garden of Eden and the Fall with the theory of the physical evolution of man? If man has evolved through many stages of bodily adaptation, how

33

can you account for the story of the Fall?'' Again, you hear us say that man was once a far more spiritual being than man of today, and that in a far-off age there were god-men on the earth; and you wonder, if god-men dwelt on earth long ago why is man still apparently at so low a state of spiritual consciousness?

'Man descended from his high estate in accordance with the divine plan. He had to undergo a process of gradual descent to inhabit a physical vehicle which in its turn had evolved from a lower state of life stage by stage until the brain had developed to such a degree that it could begin to comprehend the glory and the wonder of the God within.

'Man contains God, the Divine Essence, within his own soul. But it takes long ages for that seed of God-life to manifest through physical consciousness.

'Conceive of man in a stage of life before he came into his fuller powers of action and thought. At that time his physical body was not like the one to which you are now accustomed; for the spirit or consciousness was more outside than within the body, existing still in a higher state of life. For remember there had to be not only a process of creating a physical vehicle, but also of developing all the subtler bodies which clothe the spirit of man.

'Stage by stage not only his body, but also the mind and brain of man has evolved, until at last came the vehicle through which the divine light might descend until, in the perfect man, the full consciousness of the divine life could manifest.

'Many people, believing in the omnipotence of God, do not care to accept that there could ever be a fall of man. Yet if we look at it aright, we witness, not a depraved being falling because of knowledge of creation through the sex function but

34

rather see the process of awakening in man of his self-consciousness, leading eventually to God-consciousness. This is the whole purpose of life and evolution, this growth from unconsciousness, through self-consciousness, towards God-consciousness.

'Love of power is the basis of most of that which is called evil; desire for power which rises in the mind and asserts that self which is the lower aspect of man. So man "fell" from his perfect God-like estate, tempted by what is called evil, by his own love of power. Yet the agency of the serpent, which brought evil into the mind of man, also caused development and growth of his individual soul and mind. Evil produces individualisation, a necessary part of the process of evolution; for without this pushing forward of the self, this individualisation, there would be little urge towards growth in God's child towards the ideal of a completed, perfected son of God.

'With the implanting of the seed of evil, as man miscalls it, or of desire for self-growth, was also born within the heart of man yet another aspect of God called the Son, who represents the divine life, which is also love itself. So, while this desire for self-growth and self-expression became implanted in man's brain, or mind, and has been attributed to "evil," there was also born within man's heart that which is called love— the Son of God, the Christ, the Light whom angels worship, and even the angels of darkness bow down to—for even they are still subject to the power of love.

'Good and evil are like two wheels (which are yet one) ever at work—the higher and the lower; the action of the lower ever brings suffering, but a suffering destined to produce the perfect archetype, the perfected Christ man. Have we not told you that all men shall be raised up to the Son, shall become at-one with the radiance of the Sun?'

V

THE KING'S MEN

Man's life on earth is like a seed bed in which the divine
seed, man's spirit, is planted. His seed-casing, or husk, is
his physical body, in which his soul and spirit will live
nourished by earth experiences until that seed quickens and
responds to the spiritual sunlight coming from above. Man
in his inner self is made in God's own image. In the first
instance the Divine Mind created him perfect, but he has
since descended or strayed far from that ideal. Now he
arises to struggle again towards perfection.   W.E.

A FEW days after our visit to Dragon Hill and Wayland's
Smithy, we drove northward into the Cotswolds to visit the
Rollright Stones, which proved to be a circle of smallish
standing stones, some of which had been cracked into several
pieces by frost and weather. Separated from the main body of
the stones by the road is another, the King's Stone, some seven
feet high. Legend affirms that these stones represent a king
and his army turned to stone by a witch, and the cromlech, a
group of whispering knights who conspired against their king.
The legend is thus in line with several others, such as that of
the Dancing Maidens in Cornwall, turned to stone for pre-
suming to dance on the Sabbath. Once yearly the Rollright
circle receives a special visitation from the local villagers.

One had the impression on arrival at the circle that here
was a place which to some degree had been 'spoiled.' We
subsequently learnt that the stones had been much tampered
with by villagers and were no longer in their original position,
which may partly account for that feeling. But it did not seem

so when the message began to come through, for we felt at once the power that had been present, and the blessing. Here is the message, spoken beside the King's Stone, well away from the actual circle:

THE ROLLRIGHT STONES

According to archaeology: *the Rollright Stones comprise an unditched stone circle used for ritual purposes during the Bronze Age.*

'I feel that beneath this stone circle was a burial-place. Before this it was a ritual temple, but later races used it as a burial-place. There was once a temple of worship here. I hear the padding of feet, I feel men and women perambulating outside, and then going into a cave underground. I feel we are walking on sacred, hallowed ground.'

THE KING'S STONE—OR THE SUN STONE

According to archaeology: *a coeval monument of doubtful significance.*

'This was the point where the rays of the sun were concentrated right into the inner chamber. I hear chanting, which sounds like 'Om . . . Om . . . Om' in invocation of the sun, in worship of the sun, in calling to the sun to quicken the seed and bring forth new life. Now I can feel a sense of release from the body, of going up into the light, and that the sun's rays are shining over all this area.

'I can see a congregation of people here on midsummer's day, coming from all directions in hundreds and thousands. This sun temple was founded long ago before Britain was Britain as we know it now. There was an underground place of worship here where the brothers used to meditate and work. They also made things here; I see there was much creative activity, perhaps in the making of jewellery. Also I feel I am going through a long tunnel linking this place with another centre. I see glorious colours as though there was a concentration of etheric or planetary rays here.*

'These were not savages; they were lovely people. I see the women dressed in pure white, the men wearing tunics, with head-dresses. I can't understand the head-dresses; they are unusual, like the Norsemen wore with two horns. I think some of these people came from the north as well as the west. They also have bands round their heads—flashing stones set in gold bands. The colour predominating is a brilliant amethyst. Now I see the men dressed in ceremonial cloaks and they bring young girls bearing wheat—wheat maidens—these are perhaps indicative of the Age of Virgo.

'The King's Stone was once a central point—situated right in the centre of the sun power which was attracted to it by the ritual—this was the point from which they sent out the rays. It was both a projecting and receiving station.

'I feel there was a battle going on all the time on the etheric plane, because the dark people living in the marshes could send out astral and etheric creatures to carry out their missions of mischief. They, too, had an occult knowledge, so could do this. There was a continual pull between the forces of good and evil, which appeared as armies on the inner planes. These marsh people lived just outside the physical—in the etheric—but a very real life in etheric matter was theirs. (Here the message at the Rollright Stones ends.)

This vision may well refer to the Age of Virgo, at the beginning of a fresh sun cycle when a new race, a new outbreathing of souls, came forth.

Since the opposite sign to Virgo is Pisces, the vision of the

* This is only one of many such references in these visions.

'swamp-men' may well refer to the great ocean of psychic and elemental life out of which the new race was being born. It would be a time of a great outpouring of light and creative power, which would be used by the god-men from other planets, and those of the previous cycle who had elected to remain behind as guardians of the new race. Would these not be the hill-men, whose work would be to guard the new humanity from the 'men of the swamps,' that is to say, from the forces of darkness and chaos, possibly finding embodiment in those left behind from the great weighing up of the cycle just completed?

There would no doubt be ceremonies with the emphasis on the sowing of the corn, and the maidens with the corn sheaves would not only be symbolic but help to draw down the protective power of the Divine Mother to guard the new cycle of souls, or even perhaps to draw it forth from the dark ocean of unformed life symbolised by Pisces, opposite sign to Virgo. 'The spirit of God moved on the face of the waters.'

The reference to the creative use of sound is significant, and is only one of several such allusions we shall find as the story unfolds. It calls to mind much later experiences at Carnac in Brittany, with its huge array of stone alignments, similar to, but on a vaster scale than anything known in Britain.

We have already learnt that some form of communication existed between our 'men of the hills' and the people of Brittany, and therefore the following account of the vision at Carnac in April 1970 may all be part of the present story.

CARNAC

'Music! music!, the air was full of this powerful music and rhythm. Then the jubilant company of people gradually came into my vision colourfully clad, principally in the colours of

the sun. They performed graceful ritual dances, over and over again, mostly in circular motion, swaying, bending. Directing it all were three wise and ancient officiants.

'The whole company seemed to be under a powerful magic force. They were gay and full of laughter. I was struck by their gaiety and strength of purpose.

'At several of the menhir alignments at Menec, I immediately picked up the continuous beat of music, the air seemed to be impregnated with it. I also received the impression of a masonic order. These prehistoric people were the original masons, and I was being shown how these stone temples and alignments of stone were formed, by sound and song. The white ether which is everywhere was either the power or the substance used to create form on the physical plane.'

It would appear that these very ancient peoples, before history, had knowledge of spiritual, and indeed natural law, far beyond anything we know today. They knew of the creative power of sound and rituals; they knew of the movement of the stars, and the influence of the other planets of the solar system on the earth. Above all, they knew how to use the spiritual light and solar force. Rollright itself we learn was a centre of power for the reception and radiation of the light of solar and planetary rays for the blessing of the earth.

White Eagle says:
'Throughout the ages the light of the ancient sun brothers has been centred within, although not confined to this mystic isle, which was a sacred isle thousands upon thousands of years ago. The brethren of the ancient light travelled all over the earth, but their home was this mystic isle.

9   *The Rollright Stones* (Aerofilms Ltd.)

'If you study the inner history of your land you will come to realise that throughout the ages a tradition concerning the light of the sun has lingered in your myths and legends and folklore. When once you have studied, contemplated and meditated with greater power and understanding, you will be able to read the story of the very early sun brotherhoods who once lived here, who built temples, who worshipped here, who possessed great knowledge, not only of spiritual truth, but of physics, of the properties of matter, knowledge which was imparted to those who came seeking. We would stress how the spiritual life and influence of these god-men still lingers in your land, and in the hearts of her people. The British people are grown blind and deaf, and do not know the beautiful secrets which are hidden here. You are the inheritors of an ancient wisdom, a great light.'

VI

WE VISIT THE TRODDEN-UNDER-FOOT
CATHEDRAL

In the beginning was the Word; and that Word was a
vibration, a mighty sound which vibrated and reverberated
in an ever-widening circle. All creation is within that
circle. Think of your life as being held in a circle of light in
which you are enfolded—that you are living within that
Word, within that circle of light, and power and protection.

W.E.

SUPPOSE that some local authority suddenly decided to
drive a roadway through the middle of Westminster Abbey or
St. Paul's Cathedral, and at the same time to erect cottages
clustering round the Cathedral precincts; what an outcry
would ensue when traffic began to rumble through the sacred
building! Yet this has already happened, and is still happening,
to a cathedral perhaps more significant than either Westminster or St. Paul's. It is happening at Avebury, a temple so
vast that it would house a dozen or so Stonehenges and nearly
as many Westminster Abbeys. If you will study our picture
giving a reconstruction of how Avebury might have looked
long ago, you will glimpse something of its expanse, its
dignity, even majesty. Then compare what you see with a
present-day aerial photograph, and observe how the place has
shrunken, how its massive monoliths have been uprooted to
build the cottages which clutter up its expanse and spoil the
line of the stones' dignified array.

It will be seen how Avebury village also over-runs the
enclosure itself, while an occasional huge monolith stands in

some cottage garden—an incongruous sight. Worst of all, roads have been built right round and across the enclosure, so that now huge lorries thunder past where once the pilgrims walked and worshipped.

Yet this is still a noble place, *the* national monument of all our monuments. In a sense, its sanctity, dignity and greatness remain unimpaired, while in comparison we humans seem such trivial creatures. Like insects we cluster and defile, and like insects in a moment are gone: while Stonehenge, Avebury —they remain.

The day we chose for Avebury was one of summer's best. We had driven over early to avoid the crowds, so had the place practically to ourselves. A small herd of cows browsing among the stones gave us a placid welcome, and we settled down beside them, nearly out of earshot of the traffic, and alone except for our animal brethren. It was in conditions such as these, in peace and sunlight that the following message came through.

AVEBURY, JULY 1966

Avebury Circle is a prehistoric monument 'as much surpassing Stonehenge,' says Aubrey, 'as a cathedral doth a parish church.' According to archaeology: *the remains at Avebury consist mainly of a massive circular earthwork, $\frac{3}{4}$ mile round and about 15 feet high, with a fosse (originally 30 feet deep) on its inner side, thus suggesting a religious rather than a defensive object for the entrenchment. Fringing the inner edge of the fosse once stood a gigantic circle of unhewn megaliths and in the centre of the enclosed area were two smaller concentric circles. The largest stones weigh about 60 tons. From the circle an avenue of stones (many recently re-erected) led south-east, beyond West Kennett, to a group of small stone and timber circles called the Sanctuary, long since vanished, and now marked out on the ground.*

The message reads:

44

'The ritual here at Avebury was linked with the moon. I see a great crowd gathered to perform an elaborate ritual of obeisance to the moon, or to what I can only describe as a goddess of the moon. At that time the moon looked much bigger than it does now, and there was life on it. The people on the moon were advanced in spiritual knowledge, and a form of communication with them existed.*

'This great goddess sits enthroned as ruler of this place. The ritual here was performed under her direction, its object being the actual production of life in form—the bringing into physical manifestation of life itself, coming from the etheric world. You see, in those supremely distant times, life in wholly physical form had hardly come into being. The ancient mother-ritual, which eventually brought about the creation of life in physical form, came from Mu, the Motherland.

'This temple of Avebury was the heart and centre of all these ceremonies.

'The ritual was designed to invoke the occult, the invisible power of the gods, and then it was concentrated upon the movement of the cells and the building-up of form.

'These great stones of the temple came into physical manifestation from the etheric forms created by ritual by these people. I feel that all these stone temples in Britain were built by materialisation from etheric form.

'Now I am aware of movement, of music, harmony, sound, the music and the rhythm of the earth and the whole solar system. All are attuned, in unison. This tells me that this ancient ritual was linked with powers inherent in the solar system itself, and that the people knew how to contact outer space. All this was millions of years ago—at least, it seems to

* It could be taken that this life on the moon, like that on earth (as the vision goes on to reveal) was not yet in dense physical form.

me like millions. I can see the races come and go, come and go, come and go, while ages pass. I see a great civilisation work up to a climax and then decline. Afterwards a period follows when the land is over-run with people like savages; then yet another civilisation grows up and then another follows on.

'At one time the people living here were like the American Indian. They had red skins and appeared very tall and had a noble bearing—men today look like midgets by comparison. The grander the spirit became, the bigger grew the body. After death these people were buried in the centre (of Avebury temple) lying in a circle, with their feet to the middle, like a big clock-face might look.

'Originally this place was one of the great creative centres of this planet. The great one who once ruled here seems to me to have an immense head-dress suggestive of a crown; but its several points are like magnets attracting force and power down to them—I see sparks glittering at the points of the crown.

'Now I see that the goddess is in a procession up the avenue of stones towards Silbury Hill, and I see her enthroned on Silbury. This was an immense procession. Some of the people went before her and the rest followed. All the etheric life, such as gnomes and fairies, joined in the procession as well.

'Now I see ritual movement about an altar in the centre of a vast congregation. Perhaps the great ceremony is over.

'These standing stones at Avebury now look to me like shrunken remnants of what was once a far vaster temple. It was built in three sections—first came the inner temple, then a space and then another wall or circle of stones, again a space

10   *A reconstruction of the temple of Avebury* (Ministry of Works)

47

and then another wall and then the open sanctuary. Pillars, vast beyond belief, supported the temple. . . . I am losing my vision. . . . I am coming back. Life looks so feeble now. The village now looks like a lot of toy things set down in a haphazard way. . . .'

The foregoing message would seem to take us back into almost inconceivably remote time when it refers to the creation of physical form from etheric substance, and communication with a form of life existing on the moon at the time—which we must conceive as existing, like earth life itself, at an etheric rather than a physical level. Through ages since, the moon's influence has been subtly connected with the woman and the creation of life. Remnants and indications of mother-worship exist throughout the world, and many students of ancient monuments in Britain state that mother-worship was at one time generally accepted. In *The English Downland* H. J. Massingham suggests, 'May not Avebury have been the temple-tomb of the supreme goddess of heaven and earth, and the abodes beneath the earth, who died with the winter and was reborn with the awakening of nature?'

Rightly did the Ancient Wisdom incorporate the mother as its symbol of worship and also wisely because the same forms of worship will surely return, bringing in their train both peace and plenty. It is right that womanhood as a whole should be housekeeper entrusted with the earth's bounty; and the womb of the mother as the receptacle of life itself, created by love, has played at least as important a part in the affairs of mankind as has the male's over-eager intellect. True, the male has dominated the female for many centuries, but it has

11   *Avebury from the air* (Aerofilms Ltd.)

not always been so; and in time to come the order will again change and woman will take her rightful place as the visionary partner.

As with the vision at Wayland's Smithy, while this book was being compiled, shorthand notes of a much earlier vision received in October 1949 'by chance' came to light. There are differences between the two messages and they may well touch different strata of human experience. But there are also striking points of similarity and they tend to confirm one another, particularly since the first had lain utterly forgotten for so long. Both appear to reach far back to that Edenic period already referred to before man had been wholly bound down in matter.

AVEBURY, OCTOBER 1949

'I can see figures in flowing robes of what appears to be white ether. They come in right up the avenue of stones to this circle in which we are sitting, and circle round and round until they reach the very centre where they create a central point, like an altar, and on this altar I see a warm rosy fire. The concentration of the ceremony is on this fire. At a certain point comes an outpouring of rosy light, the warmth of the fire. Then there seems to be the manifestation of a great being. A great fountain of light rises and spreads all over the surrounding country.

'They are very big people with beautiful bodies and beautiful physique. Oh, this is a temple of magic! There are fairies and elemental beings here, uniting with the human beings. The human beings seem to be almost worshipped by these elementals as gods, and they *were* gods in those days, who had control over the elements; and they were gods because of the light which had been released in them, which they had brought with them to the earth from the invisible ethereal planets. Yes, they were god-men here.

'I think that these things happened before the earth was yet solid. It was in a more etheric and fluid state. I can hear the beat, beat, beat of these people walking solemnly, and then at a given moment the sun broke through, not the physical but the spiritual sun, broke through into the mind, into the consciousness of the people. The Great White Light! The light, the light shines! The light! The light! I can see people here sitting round as in a vast amphitheatre, watching this ceremony in the centre, and the priests and priestesses passing round and round building up this core, this centre of creative fire.

'There seems to be a nucleus right in the centre of this circle which holds everything in its course. It attracts everything to it and holds it, and I see these beings working up this power as they revolve round this central point, this core. Men were taught to concentrate on this one central point, this nucleus to which the electrons were drawn by centrifugal force. . . . The neophytes were taught the secret of moulding and moving matter by a tremendous effort of divine will, by fixing their minds securely on that one nucleus, that one central point. They could move stones, they could produce any form they wanted out of practically nothing. It was done by concentration on this central point by divine will. But there was always perfect form, always perfection, whatever they wanted to create, they had to hold that vision in their spirit, in their mind, and it gradually materialised or was brought down from the mental level to the astral and then the physical level.

'These people were god-men, they were not just of earth, they were masters from other planets. They came on rays from other planets, and these rays all seemed to converge upon central points here, in this island, in Britain. These stones, as at Stonehenge, mark the place where these cosmic or planetary rays meet. People will learn that there are these points all over the British Isles where there was a concentration of planetary rays, and at such points there is a tremendous spiritual impetus and inspiration. These points are like the chakras of the light of this mystic isle.

'This is an entrance here into the inner world, into the higher, the real world.

'Now I am getting the feeling of a mighty impact here and of the earth being pushed off its axis.* Terrific confusion. But this was not by accident, it was all in the plan to make another beginning on earth, to bring in a fresh stream of souls. There is an old world and a new world, and this new world is born in the death of the old, or, in a sense, in the crucifixion of the old. You must remember that whatever takes place in the outer or material world, also takes place in the inner world, for there is always cause and effect. The cause lies in the inner world and the invisible, and the effect is seen in the outer and the visible. Every cycle of life takes this course from the inner to the outer and from the outer back again to the inner, an in-breathing and an out-breathing. Although it might seem that this was a catastrophe, it was only a mighty manifestation, an involution and evolution; a fresh out-breathing of souls was born to set out on the new evolutionary spiral. They have gone round and round the cycles of life, just as the people process round this temple. One day our present cycle will arrive at the peak, or that central point again, the heart, the heart of the rose, the rose heart (the rose stone, as at Stonehenge), the stone where they make or made the great sacrifice,

* See Appendix, p. 113.

the great surrender, and then a burst of light, release from bondage, release from physical matter and re-birth into this eternal light. This happens to individual souls, but it also happens to the race, it happens to universes.

'All is movement, pulsation, movement, just like cell-life ever growing and increasing, and every cell which increases is almost like a life period which keeps being added to. This is a picture of eternity.

'O! It seems so strange to come back and open my eyes to the little people of earth, when I have been wandering in infinity . . .'

VII

WHEN THE ANGEL OF THE SUN
CAME OVER STONEHENGE

Ancient Wisdom teaches that behind and within the
physical sun is the spiritual sun or white light. The
ancients were taught how to use and direct this white light
for the blessing of their life on earth. They were taught
how to work with the angels to control the elements. They
had the secret of how to work within natural law to main-
tain the fertility of the soil. Some of the ancient temples
in your country were centres from which the whole country-
side was enriched by the radiation of the great white light.
                                                        W.E.

I

WHAT follows is the result of a number of visits to Stonehenge. These experiences were later combined and published
in a magazine in the form of imaginary letters which record the
gist of what was seen and heard.

The letters are supposedly written on a midsummer day
some thousands of years ago.

'Beloved,

'During the night which has passed and during the dawn
when it seemed that God Himself came down to dwell among
men, my thoughts have often flown to you. Again and again I
felt you at my side while we paced continuously through the
night around the temple of Stonehenge. At times we even
seemed to be alone together, in spite of the crowds of men
and women reaching out to the edge of the plain which sur-
rounds the temple.

'Those people had come far, some from countries across the

54

seas. I spoke with men from across the water, where they have built long avenues of stones to mark the paths of the sun.* Thousands of men and women tread these paths on occasion, chanting, singing, invoking God, so that the very soil and the gentle ethers above and within become impregnated with worship and prayer. Thereafter these are holy places, the paths of the sun.

'The pilgrims here have come from many lands, crossing the narrow seas in ships that plied to and fro. Some of the holy ones, the Priests of the Sun, come more secretly, none knowing how. It is said that with their mastery over the power of sound, by intonation and invocation their bodies become lighter than air.

'Another ancient man told me that he once saw one of the vast cross-pieces of the trilithons at Stonehenge being replaced after an earth tremor had dislodged it. (This is secret, so say nothing.) He saw the priests gather round that stone as it lay on the ground. They joined hands and marched round it chanting, then stood with arms upraised, invoking, commanding. The stone then rose apparently of its own volition, steadily as under precise direction. By now it was night and the stone shone as if lit from within, as if permeated with light. It rose, guided by those upraised commanding hands and wills until it settled back on its monster upright stones as gently as a bird. Safe back, its light shone for many hours until it gradually became again cold stone.

'I was told that the whole mighty structure of Stonehenge was raised in this way. The labour of man was used to shape the stones. This done, each upright and cross-piece weighing many tons was rendered weightless by the infusion of light and sound. Each mighty stone was then brought across the trackless

* Presumably the 'Alignments' in Brittany.

land from the quarry to the site of the temple. Even those smaller "blue" stones in the outer circle were transported in this way from the fairy-ruled mountains of Wales. The man who told me said that unbelieving people in the future would wonder at the ruins of Stonehenge, and bring out marvellous theories as to how it all happened. But the truth will be far too simple for them to understand, for they will have lost the magical powers which are now common to the Priests of the Sun.

'Before sunset came I stood on a great barrow under which kings lie buried, and viewed the scene. Already men and women had taken their places around the outer circle of stones. (The inner was kept clear by order of the priests.) The multitude reached out from that outermost ring, standing so thickly that only heads and faces could be seen. All were very still. Their very breathing was audible, so silent was the night. All were bare-footed. None spoke. Silence seemed to well up from the earth herself as if she too were aware of the blessing which was to come; as were all creatures from the lowest to the highest. Even the very birds had ceased to sing except that in the distance a nightingale carolled to the departing sun.

'For the rest, silence lay over the multitude, a multitude. which was at-one in prayer for the blessing of the Sun on all creatures and on Mother Earth herself. As we waited I believe I heard the earth breathe and sigh as if she felt the pangs of birth. And I bent down to touch the earth and bless her. Was she not Mother of men!

'The scent of the trodden earth rose sweetly. Each bruised blade of sacrificial grass gave forth its incense, and many a trodden herb in that grass breathed a richer, sharper scent.

12   *Stonehenge today* (Aerofilms Ltd.)

56

It seemed that the earth herself, the body of the earth, held sweetness; yes, sweeter than rich newly-turned soil was that savour of Mother Earth.

'Hesitating on the fringe of the crowd, and creeping among their feet, came little furry creatures of the plain and country-side, normally wild and fearful but tonight unafraid, their coats glossy from the lush herbage of June fields, bright-eyed, and tonight at-one with man.

'Night has fallen now. Try to see with my eyes and hear with me, for I long to share with you the marvels I have witnessed. I have never seen the stars more luminous or the great plain so populous with little creatures. For now the little wild creatures of the countryside gathered ever more thickly than before—the birds still on the wing (although they should have nested long before), timid animals man rarely sees—all came like pilgrims to a shrine, stealing among the standing men and women, intent on reaching the enclosed space within the outer circle of stones. Once there, without enmity, without a sign of fear of each other or even of man, they waited. As I watched, some big beast brushed against me in passing. Startled, I turned round and looked into the face of a great bear which had come wandering from the depths of far-away forests, drawn hither unconsciously by the power. Unafraid, we passed each other by.

'Then came the sound of horns, and the white-robed priests came among us, marshalling us into ranks. Let me explain that Stonehenge is built with an inner group of pairs of great up-right stones, topped with stone cross-pieces. Standing beside the upright stones are smaller "blue" stones from Wales. This inner shrine is not a true circle, but open at one end towards the sunrise. At the closed end is the rose-coloured altar stone. Around the "ring" is, first, a complete circle of "blue" stones and then another of upright stones with stone cross-pieces, enclosing the temple.* Beyond this another outermost circle, this time of wooden uprights.

'Try to picture yourself standing behind the altar stone, looking directly to where the sun will presently rise. On either side of you and behind you loom up the great trilithons, twenty or more feet high, with their attendant "blue" stones close beside them. Nothing obscures your view. You can look directly through the outer circles, then out through the wooden uprights of the outermost circle, and what do you see? You see a straight grass track marked on either side by a trench and upright stones, reaching out seemingly to the horizon (actually the distance is nothing like so great). This track marked by its rows of stones and its trenches is of primary importance—for this is called the Trackway of the Sun, and down it comes the light of the risen sun to bless the earth and all men dwelling thereon. In the middle of the Trackway, a little beyond the stone circles, is a stone on which stands a high priest to direct the ceremonies.

'Now to try to tell you how it all happened. I have told how the priests came among us with their horns to marshal us. The horns set my blood tingling to their thrilling note, but all the people were very orderly and quiet, for many had been before to the ceremony at midsummer dawn, and were already awed and prayerful. The crowd was divided; half of us were led along one side of the Trackway of the Sun out to its end, where

---

* A visitor to Stonehenge today will find most of the central 'horse-shoe' standing, with its attendant 'blue' stones. The rose-coloured altar stone has several others fallen upon it. About a third of the outer circle of stones is still standing, but of the outermost wooden circle no trace remains. Vestiges of the ancient Trackway of the Sun can be seen, now called the 'Processional Way.' This is not to be confused with the Great Ridgeway referred to earlier. The stone on which the Director of Ceremonial once stood is intact and is called the 'Hele' Stone.

the ground dipped. The other half, men, women and even children, were led out along the opposite side of the Trackway. None trod the Trackway itself on the outer journey. Immediately opposite us, over the horizon, we knew the sun would presently rise. Already we could feel its magnetic power drawing us, filling us as we all stood facing the sun. All was profoundly silent. Then the horns spoke again, not in command, but invoking the sun, praying for its beneficence. We knew what we must do then. We must absorb, fill ourselves, literally breathe in that sun.

'For human breath is magical. The priests heal with their breath; with breath expelled as sound they can raise great weights (as I have already described) or raze a building to the ground. We ordinary men and women on this night of nights were shown how to practise this magic. Of what we were told, I can say little; but we breathed in the sun's power and might. We filled ourselves with the sun's breath—for the sun also breathes; and having done so, we turned and paced slowly back in procession towards the temple, down the Trackway of the Sun, breathing-out the sun's light upon the Trackway.

'Yes, pure light! Our breath was now instinct with the power of light from the sun, and it was breathed-out in a song of power, for as we marched we sang. Our chant was controlled and led by the horns and by the choir of the priests, so that it followed one dominant pattern of song throughout, repeating and repeating itself, commencing deep down then rising, rising, rising to a great cry of triumphant joy; and by this cry we gave out, gave back all that we had received from the sun.

'And this not once, but continuing through the night! Having marched down the Trackway, when we reached the temple one half of us swung right to encircle the stone outer circle, the other half swung left to perambulate the circle of wood. Thus in two orderly circles, each turning against the other, we paced around Stonehenge, afterwards returning to the end of the Trackway to re-enact the ritual, over and over again as the hours passed. Personally, I knew no weariness. Even now I feel fresh and joyful. But I soon learned the reason why the Trackway of the Sun was so called; for as we paced down it I saw the Trackway itself and the air above it were becoming luminous with an aura of light. I looked down and saw that my feet were walking through pools of light, and indeed that all were wading through a luminous ether which clung, so that we ourselves became dimly luminous; and more, that in some way we were conveying that light down the length of the Trackway to the temple, which in its turn was becoming luminous.

'Not until then did I realise that we ourselves had become so raised in spirit that we could see things previously invisible to our mortal eyes; and that the purpose of this night of marching and chanting was to set our spirit free, so that we might see in this fashion.

'For now I saw Stonehenge revealed in its glory, the stones themselves illumined as from within. I saw the light pulsing through every stone. Each of the grey weathered uprights emitted a dull golden light, the "blue" stones a blue radiance which shone afar, the altar stone shone a deep rose. As the blood flows through the veins of a man's body so the currents of light flowed through these stones. This was so wonderful that for a time I ceased to sing and could only watch. Then more wonders unfolded, for at last I saw the reason why these "blue" stones had been brought from those faraway fairy-ridden mountains. For the stones had power to induce, to draw hither the fairies. I saw them come, I saw the little people declare themselves, made visible to man. They walked, they played, they danced among the assembled animals lighter than any thistledown, graceful as embodied air itself. These were the flower-fairies, and they brought with them the scent of flowers. They were coloured as the flowers, scented also, but more bright, more sweetly.

'There came more of the little people, some rising out of the earth itself; and others were dwarf men and gnomes which I noticed kept close to the stones and could walk through them as you or I walk through water. Stone was their habitat, I knew. These were the souls of the stones—souls which the priests had a magical power to command. Also I saw the sylphs fleeting through the darkness of the summer night.

'Beloved, not long ago I felt fresh and unwearied, but now a heaviness comes upon me. I had meant to write of the coming of the devas, of the mighty sun angels which came to make ready for the coming of the sun, and of the sun's descent to earth. Let me rest before I complete this account.

II

'Beloved, when I woke a moment ago you were closely with me. I think that my spirit has flown across the land and seas to be with you, if only for a moment, and I am sure we two are interwoven, because what I have seen during the hour of darkness and dawn has set my spirit free from its mortal chains, for these hours at least.

'Do you see the prints of an animal's feet on this letter? A hare came close to me while I slept, a beast usually so timid, but now it stands not twenty feet away completely unafraid. I

13   *A map of Stonehenge, scale about* 200 *feet to the inch, showing the Avenue which leads from the Circle.*

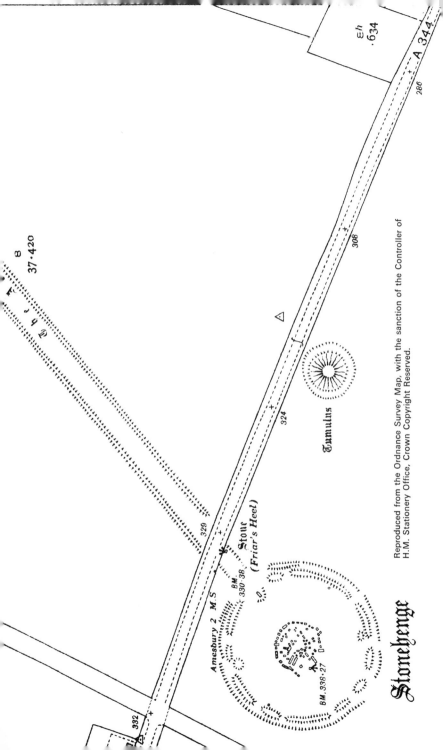

Stonehenge

Tumulus

Stone (Friar's Heel)

Amesbury 2 M.S.

BM. 330·38

BM. 338·27

37·420

634

A 344

286

308

324

329

332

saw a dog walk close to it, yet neither seemed interested in the other. So it is with us all. Peace reigns. The fears of one beast for another and their fear of man are alike stilled. Folk who have attended this ceremony before tell me that neither man nor beast will feel hunger again for several days, so richly has their being been filled by the sun. This I shall soon know. Certainly I feel no hunger so far.

'As I lie here and write, the sweet savour of the earth is all around me. It comes not only from the soil itself, with all its myriad sweet herbs, nor even is it the scent of earth brought out by the sun, as we normally know it. A heavenly essence has endowed the earth, a fragrance culled from the high clouds and the distant blue heavens golden with sunshine, an essence compounded of all blessedness and holiness brought by the dawn.

'Let me return to my story. I have told you about the Trackway of the Sun reaching out from Stonehenge direct to where the sun would rise; and of how we went out to the end of that Trackway, and there breathed in the power and light of the yet unrisen sun; and of how we then paced in procession back towards Stonehenge, all chanting and singing through the night, thereby breathing out that sunlight and power; and of how because of this, the Trackway itself became glowing with ethereal light, so that we walked through pools of light. We only saw these things revealed because we ourselves had become raised in consciousness. All would have remained hidden and ourselves blind to these wonders had we been our normal selves, I believe, for in his daily self man is imprisoned in ignorance and stupidity. But it was not so at this hour of wonder.

'For as we walked I saw men transfigured. Yes, both men and women walked as gods, freed from their clay, with shining eyes and kingly bearing; from their enkindled inner selves a light shone forth, so that we saw that God dwelt in man, and that man dwelt and walked with God in those hours before the dawn. They are so glorious to remember that I do not think that I shall ever again think meanly of my fellow creatures, having seen them thus ennobled.

'I have told you how the wild animals stole out from copse and woodland to share with man this blessing of the sun, and of how unafraid they were; and of how the little people of the fairylands were revealed by the blue light which shone from the circle of "blue" stones brought all the way from the fairy-ridden hills of Wales to Stonehenge.

'Now to tell you of the devic lords which rule over these orders of nature, for all kingdoms of nature have their controllers and all life exists under direction. There is a great stone near the temple, upon which the devic lords gather. It stands immediately outside the outer stone circle and in the Trackway of the Sun, but not directly at its centre.* All of us had been solemnly warned not to look directly upon that stone or its occupants. So we walked past with downcast eyes. Yet I dared to glance out of the corner of my eye occasionally. How could one not do so? I saw figures standing there – sometimes several, sometimes only one giant form. Some were beautiful, some fearful to look upon; some were winged beings, some were horned with pointed ears, some had cloven feet. But I saw no more than that.

'But now the night was giving way to dawn, although the sun's rim did not yet show over the edge of the earth. Now the Trackway of the Sun glowed breast high, shoulder high, head high, with its own light. We waded through light, we

---

* This massive stone is still in place but sadly weathered and is called the 'Slaughter Stone.'

breathed it in, it irradiated us. Stonehenge itself became a great temple of light, a temple roofed with light. Now we saw all things clearly. It seemed to me that I saw God and man revealed, and God's purpose with man made clear; but no words of mine can ever clothe this vision of the heart and soul.

'Now we saw the white-clad priests gather round the closed end of the inner temple. Three stood on the rose-coloured altar stone itself. Before that stone, twenty feet away, untouched by anyone throughout the whole ceremony was a heap of brushwood as high as a man, with sticks as thick as a man's finger, and butts as thick as his wrist or forearm, and all very dry.

'All this while I watched for the coming of the angels which herald the dawn. They came very quietly, very gently taking shape. At first I saw four dim forms outlined against the greying sky, yet mighty forms for all that. They stood on the outer rim of trilithons, one at the north, one at the west, one at the south, one against the glowing sky to the east, as high as the stones themselves. They stood immobile and with wings folded; and the sight was hailed with a gasp of wonder from the people, while over the rim of the world the edge of the sun appeared in an unclouded sky.

'At this supreme moment we saw the light sweep up from the sun, wave upon wave, light irradiating light across a sky glowing with gold and rose, across the wide earth. Now we saw the angelic forms more clearly as they took shape against the sky and the people began to break ranks. Unbidden, they clustered around the trilithons at the closed end of the horseshoe, behind and at the very sides of the altar stone. I stood away to the east between the sun and the temple so that I could see the angels.

'Not fifty yards away I saw the Angel of the East begin to

glow. Those of the West, the North, the South retained something of the silver-grey of the night from which they had come forth. But the Angel of the East waxed mightier than they. They were spirits of the earth, he of the sun; and as I watched I saw him becoming clothed and glowing with the sun. By now the lower edge of the sun was just over the horizon, and then I saw the Angel extend his wings until they seemed to enwrap the golden heavens. I saw his form glow ever brighter so that I shaded my eyes and bowed my head; and then . . .

'No one touched that heap of brushwood—no one went near it. I saw the priests on the altar stone extend their arms in invocation, and that moment a pillar of white flame rose straight into the air; entirely smokeless, soundless as a prayer it soared straight up, burnt silently and splendidly for a space; then sank into the earth. Yes, literally it sank into the earth. (I visited the spot afterwards—there were no ashes, no burning of the grass. It was a miracle!)

'I stood there weeping like a child. All around me men and women wept or clung together. Some lay down to kiss the earth which had become so blessed. None of us doubted that the Lord of the Sun had come down to earth to kindle that soaring flame, which had presently sunk into the earth to bless and to enkindle her. We knew, as did all the birds and beasts of the earth, that we had been greatly endowed. They knew, those women who were with child or who would conceive this year, that they were blessed and their unborn children were blessed. We knew that our harvests would be rich and plentiful. Our hearts overflowed with thankfulness; with tears of thankfulness we blessed the earth. And as we went about and walked in the blest daylight of that blest day, strangers went up to each other, grasped hands, embraced or kissed because love was so quick and powerful in their hearts . . .'

This story of Stonehenge, though of a different age and people calls to mind certain passages in Grace Cooke's *The Illumined Ones*, in which she describes her life with a brotherhood of a very ancient order in South America. The book tells of what happened when the Mayan girl, Minesta, climbed (together with her brother and the sage Hah-wah-tah, her father) to the crest of a mountain in the Andes; and how they had found hidden amid the pine trees a white temple where a mystic brotherhood lived; and how they were permitted to witness and share in the work of the inner brotherhood, how they had later stood before the altar in the inner shrine, and joined with the brotherhood in sending out the light—which was in essence their own united soul-power poured forth in a supreme effort of self-giving—and saw it directed to many communities, and also to individual men and women living in other parts of the world.

It would appear that the brothers of those ancient days in South America were not so far removed in spirit from our hill-men of Britain. Etheric vision reveals that the worship of both peoples was a form of self-giving, a literal pouring-out of self, and sometimes with almost a passion of self-surrender, for the benefit of others or for the blessing of their crops. The 'rogation,' the special blessing of their crops was crucial to these people. They were familiar with the little people of the etheric world who tended those crops, and on these, abundance depended. Insect life, bird life, animal life—all three played their part in this sowing and growing; but more essential than all was the blessing of etheric life. For everything growing has an etheric body as well as its physical self and that etheric self also needs nourishment. The little people were those appointed to watch over the crops. On their continuing goodwill and friendship much depended. Almost every primitive race throughout the world seems to have accepted this truth, judging by the world-wide myths which affirm the reality of the little people.

They had not wholly come down to earth, these ancient brothers. Their vision was as clear as ours is dulled. They saw the little people and the angels, whereas we can see nothing. The substance of their bodies had not become heavy like ours. We have descended since their day, come down and down, until we are imprisoned by the very weight of ourselves. We are still human souls, but boxed-in and cumbrous is our raiment, and while we just have to believe ourselves modern and knowledgeable, dimly we glimpse that life might be far richer were we not barred-out from Eden and become wanderers in that wilderness which is our world.

VIII

WHEN THE SERPENT ROSE
HEAVENWARD

The mystical teaching long ago established in this country
is linked with the legendary King Arthur and the brotherhood of the knights of the Round Table. . . . To each
knight is allotted two places at the table, one light and the
other dark, so each knight is represented as a dual being, one
light and the other dark, but there is nevertheless a perfect
balance and perfect equilibrium of the whole.

This symbolism teaches that every soul must strive
until these two aspects are perfectly balanced. All in the end
have to find perfect balance, equilibrium and understanding
of the value of both the positive and negative aspects of
life; must blend the two, seeing in each the wisdom of
God's law and the purpose and ultimate perfection of all
creation.

W.E.

W E now leave the chalk downs for a while, and look back to
the year 1947, when we travelled to the city of St. David's in
Pembrokeshire. North-west of St. David's and beyond the
wide stretch of Whitesands Bay, the great rocky bastion of St.
David's Head faces the sea at the most westerly point of
Wales. The coast about St. David's Head is ruggedly grand,
providing some rough and hazardous cliff walking; behind it
lies a wild area, scattered with stones large and small, and
marked in the guide-book* as ancient enclosures. There is
nothing much to sketch or photograph, only a rubbly plain,
with rubbly hills behind, and beyond the high rocky coast, a

* *History and Guide to St. David's* by Henry Evans.

70

shining sea. Dolmens, hut-circles and the like are plentiful, all left by ancient man as reminders of his life here. It was this area, these ancient enclosures and in particular the remarkable 'Serpent Circle' (to the north-east of the highest hill, Carn-llidi) which most interested my wife, who said on arrival that she saw this barren countryside as having formerly been warm and gracious, soft and gentle and full of growth and plenty. What had happened to it since she did not know, but perhaps some convulsion of nature, a rush of flood-waters or storming rains had washed the surface-soil away, leaving only rocky subsoil behind. Picture then, our little group amid the wild stones of St. David's Head, listening as the vision of the past began to unfold.

THE SERPENT CIRCLE ON ST. DAVID'S HEAD

'I see what I take to be a druid. He has white hair and rosy cheeks, a big, strong, kindly father figure. He has a staff, and on it a sign; the emblems of the zodiac are on his sash. He is holding court, blessing the people.

'I see also one who is as a queen—a beautiful, motherly woman, big in stature, of a race taller than people of today.

'The link with the Andes and Willomee* is very strong. The people are olive-skinned, darker than now. This is a fertile land with beautiful things growing in it. The people from the neighbourhood and all over the country used to come to it.

'The people bring gifts of things that they have made to the central court. They are very clever with their hands, and make most beautiful things, and with most lovely colours not obtainable today. Where are all these things gone?

'I can see that the court or inside of the palace is made of

* See *The Illumined Ones*.

gold, with lovely figures and pictures. The great feature is happiness; the feast, the joy, the dancing, the flowers.

'I feel that we could talk to the birds and animals in the same way that we do to human beings, for we all understand the same language. The trees and flowers were kindred to us, and even the grass would offer its gift. All forms of life offered their gifts.

'There was a battle between good and evil leaders, and the good withdrew, but are waiting to take over and teach the children, their descendants, how to regain the kingdom. The children follow their own way, they wander in the wilderness for a period until the rebirth of a new age. What happens to individuals happens also to whole races and even to worlds. All life moves in cycles.

'These were descendants of the ancient people who came from Hyperborea—the original people of this earth planet. The pure sun-life has gone back into the earth, into the great caves. In those days the sacred magical fire was kept burning from one solstice to the other; brought down from on high, it never went out. It was life to the people. I can now see great pacings round and round and round, and on and on. Beautiful was the feeling as we paced the serpent-trail, the wisdom-trail. This perambulation had an effect on our whole being physically, mentally, etherically and spiritually.

'People used to make pilgrimages here from Egypt, from the east, from the west. The Egyptians came here for the wisdom and took it back to their sun-baked land. What remains here —the stones that you see overthrown, are meaningless to the blind, but contain the eternal wisdom to those whose eyes are opened. These stones are older than any of the Egyptian

14 *St. David's Head* (Aerofilms Ltd.)

temples, yes, older than the great pyramid itself. This spot is more ancient than Stonehenge. Stonehenge is a later erection after the flood.

These centres can be found across Britain from south to north in the form of a vast cross. But the line is more to the west than the east.

The following is another account written down afterwards by Grace Cooke, from notes taken on a different occasion at St. David's Head in July 1947.

'My inner vision opened and I saw the ceremony of serpent-worship taking place. I saw that great numbers of people by their perambulation in a large circle right round the valley (the site lay in a kind of flat valley) were creating circles of light, on the etheric plane just above them; as the perambulation proceeded the spiritual power rose and increased. From the centre of the circle made by the human figures, a line of light arose which moved in a spiral, keeping pace with, or rather, quickening the human figures as they perambulated. Then as I watched, the spiral of light thus generated began to rise from the valley high up to the heavens, increasing in size and radiance as it rose. And at the top of the spiral—which now resembled a rising serpent—there formed a blazing light in shape like a sun, full of colour, and sending forth rays which now extended over and blessed the adjacent lands—that is, as far as my vision of the lands went.

'This explained to me the true inner working and purpose which had inspired and was behind the serpent-worship. I was told that later this ceremony had become corrupt in some lands, taking form as a kind of black magic, so that participants only succeeded in arousing the sexual fire of kundalini in man. It was this debasing of the power which brought eventual destruction to various civilisations which in the beginning had been instructed by god-men how to use the power of the white light. One still senses the grey remnants left on the etheric plane by such rituals. In the new age man's intellectual pride and arrogance must be eradicated if mankind is to regain contact with the true spiritual life forces. It is the grey mental world which is the real enemy of mankind.

'Nevertheless, my teachers said that it would be incorrect for us to interpret the "fall" or "descent" of the human race as contrary to the divine plan; for only through experiencing or undergoing the lessons of life both good and bad while on earth can man or woman attain to the perfect balance which must be held between human and divine life; as was exemplified by Jesus.

'This sacred white light was once understood as being the very life force of our race; a time must come when this spiritual creative force will be better understood by our people, for it is their veritable life-essence.

ST. NON'S WELL

'To the inner eye the neighbourhood of St. David's is bespangled with points of light shining like stars in the night sky. At each of these centres I saw ancient spirits, both human and of the elemental type.

'Due south of St. David's lies the little sheltered cove of St. Non, and in a field above can be found the ruins of St. Non's Chapel which marks the spot where St. David is said to have been born.

'When I was meditating by St. Non's Well I became aware of the presence of a beautiful woman, who seemed the very personification of perfect motherhood. To look upon the brightness of her face and raiment was like trying to look straight into the sun—it was far too bright for me to gaze upon ; but I still remained aware of her presence and of the marvellous holy power she radiated. Then two further figures appeared. My impression was that one of them was St. Michael with the flaming sword of truth unsheathed, and that the other was St. John, bearing the scroll of the New Church, to which will presently be entrusted the secret of creation and the true story of the Garden of Eden.

'I learnt in my vision that in the beginning, when human life first came, the earth was created in perfect balance. I was told that life started in the Hyperborean regions of the earth, and that what is now Great Britain was part of the first home of humanity. In those days it was like a garden of paradise. The land was fertile, the sun above warm and life-giving; there were many kinds of fruits, and rich grasslands on which kindly animals fed. These were never exploited in order to satisfy the greed of man, because in those days there was no greed. This was a land 'flowing with milk and honey'—and so it continued for a while, until the testing by the forces of evil came, and many succumbed, tempted by lust for power. Thus there were two groups; on the one hand those who under Lucifer left the paradise which had been theirs and descended into a wilderness of coarser bodies and lives of hard work and struggle spent in matter; and on the other, the still gentle and kindly white brethren who lived under the direction of their lord the sun-king.

'The messenger repeated that Britain was the first home of these ancient white brothers. Although most of them are now withdrawn from sight they still dwell in the hills and in lonely places removed from the conflict of earth. They know that Britain can rise again with their help. So the white brothers

linger on, patiently watching and waiting for men to turn
away from false gods towards the pure light of the gentle ones.

ARTHUR'S COIT

'At sunset one day, while near Arthur's Coit, a great
cromlech close by St. David's Head, I seemed to see right
through the earth and rocks and beheld an assembly of the
white brethren, wise men of noble countenance, counselling
with each other about the future of mankind. The brethren
then conveyed to me that they belonged to a race preceding
the advent of our present humanity. They had witnessed the
downfall of Atlantis* which, they said, was due to the over-
powering mental development of the Atlantean priesthood,
who had possessed highly developed occult power which they
used for selfish ends. This misapplication of spiritual power
caused the earth to attract to itself a body from outer space.†
This cataclysm struck the earth thousands upon thousands of
years ago, and may well have inspired the story of the fall of
man and the subsequent closing of the gates of Eden. Humanity
became completely clothed in the densest matter, and has now
reached the lowest point of the path it then took, the lowest
depths in its imprisonment in heaviness and limitation. However the brothers also spoke of a future of freedom brighter far
than man of today can ever glimpse.

'Centres of the ancient brotherhood have been established
in many countries, but will remain unknown and invisible
because they function in a higher dimension than humanity
does. Nevertheless, they are as real as this world is, and the
ancient ones can and will slow down the vibration of the ether
in which they exist until it merges into physical matter. This is

---

* See Appendix, p. 110.　　　　　† See Appendix, p. 113.

how the ancient brethren will come among us again in the New Age, ready to impart their secrets to those who can understand.

'The brothers also spoke about the method of transit employed on Atlantis, which was by levitation and projection across space—a method as natural to men in those days as walking is to us today. Communication between the various groups of brethren held no difficulty because a messenger could be sent from Britain to Atlantis, or to the Andes, or to the Himalayas in a matter of seconds. One method was for the initiate to retire into a chamber in the temple high on the mountains. There he would compose himself as if for sleep and in a few seconds his bodily form would dissolve and vanish from sight, and immediately afterwards would appear among the particular brotherhood to which he had been sent. The brothers assured me that this means of communication would be used again and that when mankind was more advanced spiritually it would be able to enter into communication with other planets in this way.

FOEL ERYR

'Another place of magic lies in the Prescelly Hills. Resting on a large flat stone on the summit of Foel Eryr, one of the highest of this range, I was almost in another world, and in that higher state of consciousness, I was again visited by an ancient one, who looked ageless and stood half as high again as present-day man. He wore a long white flowing beard, and his deep violet eyes were shining with compassion. Also they held a humorous twinkle and conveyed a wide understanding. Indeed, this man inspired a confidence and peace of spirit beyond words of mine to describe.

'His flowing white robe and golden crown suggested kingship, and were I think a symbol of his true authority. I questioned: Could this be the spirit of Britain or some ancient king of Britain—perhaps Ar-Thor, whose presence had remained here in this mystic isle to help his people to rise again from their dead past to inherit a new golden age? As I waited before this noble figure I felt bathed again and again in golden light. I felt his warmth of blessing, and the mountain-side faded entirely from my consciousness.

'Now the vision changed, and there seemed something strangely familiar about the figures I now saw gathered in a temple similar to a Grecian building, but not of the type with which we are familiar today. I noticed how the columns rose from the golden mosaic floor to support the very high domed translucent roof. Here again a ceremony of the white brethren was taking place, not unlike that which I had seen in the Serpent Circle at St. David's Head.

'I saw that the perambulating brothers were clothed in drapery fastened on each shoulder with a jewelled clasp and underneath this I could see the outline of a tunic, such as the Greeks wore; the women wore flowing white robes girdled with gold, and across and under the breasts was a golden cord; and fastened to each shoulder was the flowing cloak. They wore long hair coiled at the nape of the neck and the head was decorated with the familiar gold band. (Could this have been a vision of a later age?)

'The significance of the partnership between the men and women of the brotherhood was now impressed on me. For in this perambulation the whole company became exactly and perfectly balanced; the male and female, the positive and negative life-streams were mingled and made one; and again I saw the golden serpent of light arise from the assembled brethren, its head at length disappearing from sight beyond the opalescent dome of the temple.'

These visions at St. David's (which occur before those on the downland) are clear and powerful, and help to elucidate or underline much that has gone before. They speak of the perpetual battle between the good and evil powers, of the corruption of the pure white magic by desire for power and gratification of the lower self. They give a picture of the two paths—of humanity gradually degenerating because of the domination of the lower self, coming right down into matter, into coarse bodies of flesh, to experience sorrow and travail and eventually gain wisdom; and of those other pure white brothers, and particularly the mighty and beautiful Ar-Thor, who remain just beyond the veil, in the white ether, waiting to help men rise and 'return to their Father,' but all the time pouring out their love and wisdom on mankind.

We understand too that all these happenings recounted belong largely to what is referred to as an 'earlier humanity,' before Atlantis was submerged in some great cataclysm brought about by men's misuse of the power entrusted to them.

Through it we see the theme of the timeless brotherhood who from age to age, from one race to another, have guided and sustained earth's humanity.

White Eagle says:
'You will ask, "If this beauty once existed on the earth why is it that it is now finished and that we are living, as you tell us, like savages?" Because the priests who received their knowledge from the great Sun Brotherhood found that they could use magical secrets to give them dominion over their

fellows. Implanted in all of us are the two aspects of positive and negative; good and evil. Man has the gift of freewill, and can respond to the desire on the one hand for power and dominion, or, on the other, for love and wisdom for the blessing of his fellows. Some of the ancient peoples allowed their desire for power to overcome the wisdom of love. They used their power unwisely. When the balance between light and darkness is not held the equilibrium of the earth is disturbed and it brings catastrophe.

'Some of you believe that at some time a body from outer space, falling upon the earth, brought widespread destruction through earthquake and flood.* The Bible tells how Noah was warned, and built an ark to shelter his chosen ones against the flood. Other similar stories containing elements of truth are to be found in the religious history of a number of races. There was such a catastrophe, brought about by misuse of magical power, misuse of God-power. You will ask why God allowed such happenings? We are not ready yet to give you the answer to this question because you are not ready to receive it, but we ask you to believe that there is a profound spiritual reason why catastrophe was drawn to the earth, and that the eventual outcome will be in the spiritual evolution of humanity. Recognise the omnipotence of your Creator, remembering that God is all wise and loving. Therefore whatever comes in the form of catastrophe, pain or sorrow is the result of man's misuse of a magical power and is not visited upon him by a cruel and jealous God.

'According to the purity of man's life and motives after he has gained knowledge of this creative power, man draws to himself good or evil, individually or collectively. Thus the impact with the earth was brought about through the magical

* See Appendix, p. 112.

practices of those who endeavoured to use for selfish ends the secret of the power confided to them by their wise elder brethren. Since then there has been a re-forming of the crust of the earth. What we want to get home to you is that buried still in those regions is this ancient light and power which can only be released spiritually. The spirit within man is part of the spirit which is God. The spirit of God in man has to grow, to be awakened, to be fostered. The little man has to stand in reverence and in obedience to that divine light, that divine urge. He must learn to apply that light before anything else in his life, before everything which is done—individually or nationally or internationally. Then will the light and power imprisoned within the very stones of the earth be released.

'Dwell on the light. Dwell on spiritual substance. Think of beauty. Think of the light beautifying, perfecting all form. You do no good by dwelling on misery and horror. Strive to attain a degree of love and sympathy, but do not descend into the pit. You cannot help your brother man thus. In the spheres of light, when the messengers go forth to help the bound and fallen, they gently raise them, bringing them out of the darkness into the light. This is what you must do even in your limited way. You must raise the consciousness of the peoples. Do not be drawn down into the pit of misery and the vortex of ugliness. You must concentrate always on happiness and harmony. Always, always know that good is the first principle of life; and when man will respond to the direction which his own heart gives he will leave behind all the ugliness, the pain and sorrow, and beautify the earth, as God intends it to be beautified, by his own spiritual and creative effort.'

IX

MAIDEN OF THE HIGH HILLS

What religion might do to help mankind is to break down
the barriers and to fling aside the shrouding curtains of
materialism; so that man could feel and know for himself
that there is no death; and that his life is planned as part
of a vast plan for the gradual emancipation of humanity;
and that no man can ever do wrong to any of his fellows
without in time suffering the exact measure of pain he
himself had formerly inflicted.   W.E.

We are now back among the English downland, and staying
in Dorchester, our plan being to visit Maiden Castle, situated
a mile or so to the south of the city. No aerial photograph, no
attempted pictorial reconstruction can do justice to this
heroic spot. It is one of the largest, the most formidable earth-
works in Britain, too majestic to confine on paper or on
canvas. Its base covers approximately 47 acres, while its
boundaries (for the site consists of a vast flat-topped hill) are
so deeply entrenched with triple trenches that it requires
some hardihood to descend and surmount them. In their prime
those entrenchments must have been twice their present
depth and height and guarded against attack by barriers of
thorn.

Briefly, the present Maiden Castle seems to have been built
as a permanent fortress or camp to shelter not only peoples but
also their cattle and sheep. To this end its several entries or
posterns are ingeniously designed to repel an enemy attack, and
when defended courageously could prove almost impregnable.
Many and bloody battles must have taken place on this spot.

83

It is no part of our theme to recall these ancient battles. Rather would we tell of our experience in this day and age when we climbed the ramparts and reached the great hill-crown spread over many acres; recalling that across those acres it was heavenly to walk, heavenly to sink down, to bury one's face in the short sweet grass, to feel the springy turf support one's body, to hear the earth herself breathe, and feel the beating of her heart; heavenly to hear the lilting song of the lark as he rose ever higher in the sky; and to savour the thyme and other herbs impregnating the grass-lands so sweetly and so purely with their fragrance. Never was a place so little soiled by man as this, for some pure essence has cleansed all harshness away, silenced all clamour, all viciousness, and buried old-time cruelty under the forgiving soil. Here Britain becomes her visioned self, ennobled, steadfast, strong; and from here power and blessing reaches out to endow those sons of Britain who are receptive, with a like strength and stead-fastness. And as we lay thinking, and responding to that power and blessing, we knew the heart of Britain still to be strong and resolute.

Here, on this height, holiness, purity and blessing comes welling out of the earth; and as it rises it would raise Britain so that she may reclaim her great heritage of spiritual leader-ship of the world. We saw her potential, and the rich service her people might some day render to the world. Soon must come the time when our poor world must incline to the ways of peace—to a sounder, a more reassuring peace than the nations have yet devised. None has the vision or the power to incline the minds of other nations towards peace that Britain might have. For deep down the powers whisper into the heart of Britain—while upon her heights the larks sing high and clear, and the sweetest air in all the world blows across them.

They speak, those dead men of old who are forever living, forever labouring, of the mighty charge laid on Britain. Nor do they ever falter or despair, the ancient ones, when we ignore them or question their reality or their mission. They know that some day a new generation will arise who will listen and become illumined.

It will be seen by the message spoken on that summer day in 1966 how gradually its theme stands clear, as it were; first came the murky part, the mention of cruelties and conflict still impressed on the ether. Excavations at Maiden Castle corroborate those conflicts; and the relics on exhibition at Dorchester museum testify to the many generations which have lived and fought within the castle ramparts. Our message pierces through all these by degrees, and presently comes to earlier, purer days. Sometimes at a jump it leaps from perhaps a few thousand years ago to twenty, fifty thousand, half a million years ago, and we have no means of assessing the time-gap which separates the 'then' from the 'now.'

HARD BY MAIDEN CASTLE

According to archaeology: *Maiden Castle is a causewayed enclosure, long mound hill-fort and Roman temple. Neolithic, Iron Age and Bronze Age.*

'I can see a lot of people come here up a river, travelling by row and sail boats. The boats have one mast leaning almost horizontally across the boat. The people are dark-skinned, perhaps from the Mediterranean area. They seem to have come here seeking for some metal, perhaps copper or gold.

'Before this time, when many people landed on this shore, I see that the countryside was very fair and beautiful. Gentle people lived here. It was a place of the white light—a paradise.

They were simple, religious people who worshipped the Giver of Life, Mother Earth, whose bounty gave them their crops. I can see a good deal of water lying about in this area. These people built their houses of mud or clay, and not of stone. I can see houses covered with flowering vines, and near by ran a river where fish were caught. The people were beautiful, but not very big in stature.

'After this peaceful settlement bands of marauders came down from the north east; the simple people were over-run, and their civilisation lapsed into savagery. Then I can see armies and soldiers coming—I see the sunlight glinting on their helmets and shields. Over their armour they wore cloaks, and were obviously wealthy people. These in turn took possession of the land, but finally sailed away.

'The early people were very devout; they worshipped the sun and the white spiritual light which emanated from the sun.

'I see that there was once a hill near where we stand, like Silbury Hill, which was an altar for these early people. They knew about both astrology and astronomy. I can see their women working in an encampment. They are dyeing wool in bowls or vats on the ground. I can see big strands of wool hanging up to dry. I see long lines of wattle fencing and wattle huts plastered with mud.

'These people were undoubtedly Sun and Divine Mother worshippers.

'Now I can see big flying machines arriving here, people flew direct from Atlantis or America. This was once an important centre and even a capital, much bigger then than today. I can see back to a time when visitors from other planets came here.

'These gentle people could not exactly be called "simple" because they had much knowledge, but not of an intellectual nature. They knew the secret mysteries of the elements, and the inner worlds. These were the very earliest people here; they were before any of the others mentioned previously. They were the real, the earliest of all in this country; they came from a continent now lost. There is a wonderful history behind the British people if only they will dig deep enough down to find the record of the pure lives of these people.

'After this pure civilisation came war, bloodshed and much cruelty to both men and animals, but this happened much later. The early people were good and noble.

'I can see that at one time Dorchester was a great port of entry into Britain, it was right on the coast. When people voyaged by sea, they landed here. Emigrants came to these lands from the lost continents.

MAIDEN CASTLE ITSELF

'I feel that this was originally a temple of sun worship for the early people who came from Atlantis. Only later did it become a fort. I feel there are particular parts of Britain and the rest of the world, where certain cosmic rays are focused. Here the ancients (with their knowledge of astrology and astronomy) built their temples. There is a wonderful feeling of being half-way to heaven. I think these sun temples were not only for the worship of God, but also served as observatories to watch the stars.

'Gods and spirits referred to in mythology were once all real spirits. I contact a sun-god messenger. The glittering shield he wore was meant to portray the development of the heart-centre—a blazing golden centre. God-men such as these came to this place from outer space. They were so highly evolved that their own heart-centre shone out in this way.'

Our readers must feel that we have hitherto evaded dealing with either the 'visitors' from outer space mentioned in our messages, or with the frequent references to Atlantis. Everyone must form his or her own opinion regarding visitants from planetary worlds, since none of us has much to go upon.

Atlantis, however, comes into a different category, for we have here tangible evidence supporting the various myths which recall this land and its demise beneath the waves. If such a land existed, we should expect some traces of it to remain, and some indication of its contribution to civilisation. All great nations leave an imprint, a heritage for future generations.

Has Atlantis left any record, say, on the floor of the Atlantic, any traces of her mighty temples and cities? Some fifty years ago, one Ignatius Donnelly set himself to investigate the facts of the case, facts which he later set forth in his book *Atlantis* which, remarkably enough, people have been reading and discussing ever since, to an extent which has necessitated a recent paper-back reprint.

Mr. Donnelly's idea was that if Atlantis had really existed as a considerable continent situated in mid-Atlantic, its influence and culture would have certainly reached to its east and west shores (such as those of South America, Europe and Africa,) and that countries on both sides of the Atlantic would retain Atlantean traces. Such traces if found to be similar would certainly support the idea that a linking continent had once existed.

When my wife was a child, she dreamt that she frequently travelled by an airship which sped through the skies with complete mastery; and that she had embarked by going up to

15   *Maiden Castle* (Aerofilms Ltd.)

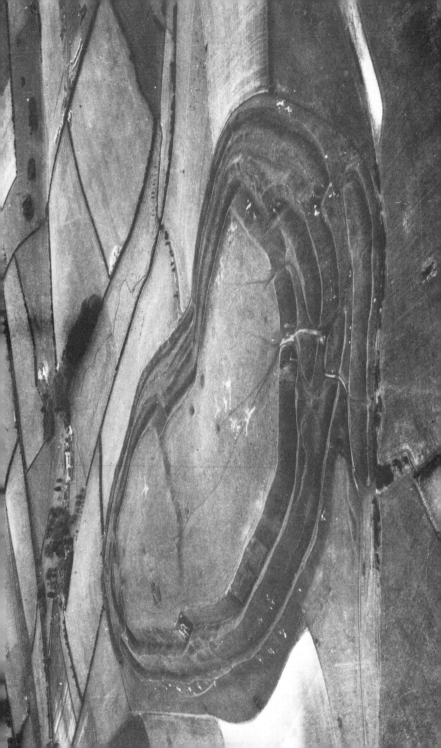

wait at the top of a metallic tower. When the aircraft arrived it was moored to the tower for her to embark, and at journey's end she disembarked in the same way. She undertook not one journey but many during her childhood dreams.

However, Donnelly's book has little to do with dreams. Facts are what this author is after, and to this end he scoured coasts and continents to the north, south, east and west of former Atlantis. Did they build alike in both South America and Egypt? Yes, they did. Was their reverence and concern for their dead expressed in much the same way by construction of pyramids? Yes, their burial customs were alike. Did Egyptian and South American styles of house-building tally in any way, making allowance for differences in climate and availability of building materials? Yes. Did their respective means of expression in speech, picture-writing, painting, carving, pottery—in the thousand ways a civilisation expresses itself—did these tally? Yes, many did. Then what about the animals, birds, insects, plants, herbs, trees? Did similar kinds manifest on both sides of the Atlantic Ocean, and if they did, had they not been planted and acclimatised there by the voyagers from Atlantis? It might well be. How far then did the religions of the east and west peoples correspond, their knowledge of the stars and their courses, the calendars by which they ascertained their time of year, season and day? Yes, indeed, in all of these correspondences were found, often very marked.

The cumulative evidence in the book proves almost over-whelming. Moreover, after reading it the reader must readjust some of his ideas. He need no longer believe that the ancients were split up into separate communities holding sparse inter-course. Instead, they were great seamen and voyagers. Maybe they mastered the skies as well as the seas. Ancient books record many a myth telling of arrivals and departures through the skies; and if this all happened during an Edenic age when earthly matter had not become so heavy, dogged and intractible, air and sea travel would have been that much easier and safer.

It will be seen that the several novel and sometimes startling notions which our messages have introduced begin gradually to fall into place. In our Avebury messages we went back to some far earlier age when matter itself as we know it was only in process of formation. What we should now hold firmly in mind is that religion also had become interchangeable, universal, with the ancients. Variations in faith or belief were mostly local, mainly superficial. Beneath all was a natural religion world-wide in scope, based on no book nor on the teachings of one man, a religion appertaining only to the Earthly Mother and the Heavenly Father. Both east and west knelt to serve these Two. The Mayan girl, the hill-man of Britain might well have knelt in prayer together and found no shadow of variance; while during all their fleeting years their Earthly Mother sent her Angels of Air, Water, Fire and Earth faithfully to serve them, while their Heavenly Father above, ruling the intercoursing heavens, held them in His close blessing. His power was immanent in their lives, so that when they affirmed that 'The Heavenly Father and I are One' they also lived their lives in Him.

X

RELIGION PURE AND UNDEFILED

How will the divine in man worship in the New Age? By
the aid and authority of some great new Church—inspired
and renewed, organised and world-wide? No. The
wisdom brought to men millions of years ago was never
meant for the lips, rested on no authority, called for no
priesthood, but dwelt in the heart. I see in the future that
the brotherhoods to come will meet in temples, or places
sanctified to God by grace and power, to worship by the
outpouring of their hearts, in silence, in love to all. I see
more, for these true brethren will be in contact with the
planes unseen, and draw therefrom powers great and
potent. There is no limit, no horizon to the vista; fair
and broad the whole earth opens to the sunlight of God. I
see no barrier between man and Christ; and Christ, the
King of Kings, with his people; yes, with wondering eyes
I behold that Second Coming.   W.E.

L ET us incline our eyes and hearts again unto the hills, whence
comes the light, and where we can again become alone with
ourselves. For we are seeking straightness of vision, wholeness,
some measure of wisdom. Our human structure so quickly and
easily gets broken down in towns. But once out in the open
and blessed downlands we can breathe in expanse, and our little
beings can reach towards infinity, can inhale truth concerning
ourselves and all the deeper issues of our being.

Massingham writes in The English Downland:
'. . . standing (on Inkpen and Winkelbury and Bulbarrow,
on Eggardon and on Windover) with only my feet on solid

earth and the rest of me awash in space, islanded in the past, I have at times felt my pulse quicken with something that was not an exulting in the high places. It was fear, fear of the loneliness and vastness and majesty of the scene, the fear of a child of the Machine Age. . . . It has been with contrary feelings that I have passed day after day wandering the downy solitudes, thankfulness that I was able to escape for a time from the anxieties and tribulations our period rivets upon all of us alike, and regret that there are so few to whom the half-heavenly inheritance of the English downs is anything but a name. It remains a fact that for every thousand people who know and use the roads across the downs, there are not ten who ever set foot upon them.'

But you and I are going to be numbered among the ten. Let us again in thought stand on Maiden Castle. About us is wide expanse, with no room for littleness. The so-called 'mighty dead' are close beside us, all around us, very gently, quietly living with us, still whispering, telling of their kindly being. What manner of faith sustained these men and women, making their lives so rich in God?

For this we have to turn to records left as an endowment to mankind by the brotherhood of the ancient Essenes. Before we study their writing, however, we have to realise both that the Essene faith was of a very ancient origin, and as already suggested that a far closer touch and intercourse was once maintained between countries than is generally believed. People of Atlantis unknown to us now may have utilised means of navigation both by sea and air, the Indians of America may have frequently sailed the Atlantic, with Atlantis as a central haven at which to call. We just don't know, but in those days religion may have spread the world over. We know for a fact that long ago people could drive their cattle and sheep across what is now the English Channel. In short, the ancient brotherhood teaching can be claimed by no one race or country. It was a concept held and lived by many peoples the world over.

Essenes in the widest sense do not belong to any one period of time, for their teachings are universal in their application and ageless in their wisdom. Traces of the ancient teaching appear in almost every country and religion of antiquity. Fragments of it are found in Sumerian hieroglyphics and on tiles and stones dating back some eight or ten thousand years ago. And these fragments appear to stem from an even earlier period. The same fundamental principles are discoverable in the Zend Avesta of Zoroaster, in the teachings of Buddha, in the Vedas and Upanishads, in the Tibetan Wheel of Life, and in the Law of Moses. The Essene traditions were known in ancient Egypt and among the Greek Pythagoreans and in Palestine and Syria. Josephus Flavius, the celebrated Jewish historian, described the Essenes as 'a race by themselves, more remarkable than any other in the world' and declares the teaching to be perpetuated through an immense space of ages.

Dr. Edmund Bordeaux Szekely has made it almost his life's work to study and present the Essene tradition to the world, having from 1927 to 1947 searched the works of the ancient historians and philosophers, together with manuscripts in the library of the Vatican, the library of the Hapsburgs in Vienna, and that of the British Museum. He dedicates the book which incorporates the results of this arduous search, 'To all those who perceive that peace for the whole depends on the effort of the individual.'

The book in question, published in 1957, is *The Teachings of the Essenes from Enoch to the Dead Sea Scrolls*, and it is published in San Diego, California, but copies are obtainable from a London publisher, C. W. Daniel & Co. Ltd.

According to Dr. Szekely a central feature of the Essene tradition is what is called 'angelology'—rather a clumsy word. They not only believed with all their hearts in the reality of angels, but also worked with and beside them. Every day at dawn they entered into communion with some specified angel representing *earthly* forces and powers. This is how they expressed devotion to their 'Earthly Mother,' a conception they held in deep reverence, almost in awe. With each dawn they summoned an earthly angel with like reverence and awe. It was deemed sinful to fail in their communion and they spoke a preamble before each communion, enjoining reverence.

They called first, on the first day of the week (Saturday), upon the Earthly Mother, contemplating all the sub-products of Mother Earth, feeling the currents of the Earthly Mother flowing into them. On the second day of the week they evoked the 'Angel of Earth'—of generation and regeneration. While voicing that name, the Essene thought about the fertility of all growing things, about the stored-away life force in the top-soil of the earth; he thought of growing grass and blooming flowers. Together with the summoning of the Angel of Earth he also mentally summoned the life-force out of the earth—doing this with authority, almost with command, and feeling that same life-force flowing through his body, renewing, regenerating its health, power, well-being.

On the third day, after voicing the preamble with reverence, he called the Angel of Life, again with authority, and felt its power enter into him, while he thought about the life-force or vitality stored in trees and forests, and drew upon that life-force to revitalise his body, and indeed his whole being.

On the fourth day he summoned to him the Angel of Joy,

while thinking about all the joy welling up, manifested in nature's flowers, in the song of her birds, in bright clouds above, in sunshine, in the beauty of dawn and sunset; so that while drawing joy to himself from all of these he also drew closer to his Earthly Mother, feeling anew her loving care for her child.

On the fifth day he summoned the Angel of the Sun, thinking about the rising sun, and feeling the inflow of warm sunlight enter him, the point of entry being his solar plexus, from whence warmth and light irradiated his being. The sixth day was in turn dedicated to the Angel of Water, when the Essene thought about seas, lakes, rivers and falling rain, the rising sap in trees, and identified his own blood with pure water flowing, coursing through every vein, purifying his whole bloodstream. The seventh day was set apart for the Angel of the Air. As always, after the preamble, with reverence he summoned this angel, all the while breathing rhythmically, and felt its power enter into his lungs, filling his being and renewing him.

Therefore seven mornings each week, never missing a day, the Essene communed with his Earthly Mother and her angels, in course of time growing to love and venerate her the more, becoming ever more conscious of the blessings she bestowed on him. His daily communion taught him his utter dependence upon that Earthly Mother for every need. She was his warmth, constant in care and watchfulness over him and hers; and to express devotion he tended his crops, his herds and all living creatures with loving care.

An acute change of heart divides that day of life and this present era. Mother Earth nowadays is desecrated by artificial fertilisers, poisoned by sprays which kill her birds and other humble creatures and eventually wash down into the seas which encircle the globe, deforming and destroying even the fishes and the sea birds which feed on them; she is impoverished by greedy cropping. Dare we also recall our factory-farming, with its afflicted and tortured animals and birds? Better not to think too much, perhaps, although every feeling of revulsion on our part hastens the day when these horrors will cease.

What effect did these communions produce on the Essene brother? A decisive answer is to hand. The Essenes lived long and healthy lives, with an average life-span of one hundred and twenty years—which is probably man's rightful allocation of years on earth. The historians were amazed by the Essenes' resistance to pain, illness, weariness. Paramount was the purity of their habits of life; their whole living proved responsive in all ways to their faith.

When dusk fell, they turned to their Heavenly Father. Evening was dedicated, not to the earthly angels but to the heavenly—in succession each evening to the Angel of Eternal Life; the Angel of Creative Work; the Angel of Peace; the Angel of Power; the Angel of Love; the Angel of Wisdom; and then on the last day of their week they communed again with their Heavenly Father, asserting 'the Heavenly Father and I are One.'

We shall not examine these heavenly communions at any length. Civilisation has clipped our wings, so we cannot flutter very high or far. But our vision is not imprisoned. We can still gaze skywards and perchance see truth soar above us like a white-winged bird; see that in this worship of the Earthly Mother side by side with the Heavenly Father we are offered religion pure and undefiled. A religion inscribed across the largess of our earth, with a span broader than the oceans and higher than the skies, embracing both heaven and earth. A religion not confined to any scripture, nor tied to happenings

97

of two thousand nor of ten thousand years ago as the last word of truth ever to be voiced. With each dawning it becomes renewed, for he who communes with the angels at each dawn and dusk finds that angel enters deeply and abides with him—enters into his subconscious from whence it uprises and expresses itself in daily life.

The Essenes held that the planets and other universes beyond our own were also imbued with life-force. They believed that life filled all space, was often incorporated in greater and wiser beings than human kind. Also they conceived all the universes as ever dependent on the operation of what they called the Great Law—so great a law that it comprehended all lesser laws of man and nature. They visualised this law as ever operative, ever wise and far seeing, aware of everything that happened and ever expressing a great heart of kindness. To help their understanding, they visualised the law as taking the form of a tree. Downwards into the earth surrounding it reached seven roots; upwards into the heavens seven branches. The former represented the seven earthly angels, the latter the heavenly angels. At its centre, spaced midway between earth and heaven sat the Essene brother, deep in meditation, all his bodily being nourished and sustained by the earthly angels, all his soul and spirit quickened and illumined by the heavenly.

This, then, was his conception of the realities of the universe in which he found himself established. He regarded the universe as an infinite and eternal garden created and sustained by the Heavenly Father and (so far as earth is concerned) by the Earthly Mother. By so doing he identified his nature with that of the great simplicities. That is to say he saw no harshness on the part of the Lord in the world about him; he believed in an ordered world. If people around him suffered, if he himself had to suffer, they as well as he but reaped as they once had sowed. He looked with compassion on all living things, feeling that each was his brother, from man down to the least of creatures. He could not bring himself to kill or inflict hurt upon any one of them. He ate only the simplest foods, but also loved to grow those foods; for then they became his children, a part of his household and family living in the infinite and eternal garden.

He lived long, and died not because of ill health or senility but because his time had come to enter into yet another aspect of the garden. He lived within the shelter and embrace of the knowledge of this Great Law. Perhaps he had only glimmerings of knowledge, but even then sufficient to simplify him, to induce in him purity of living and ready affection for all his fellow creatures.

As already stated traces of this Essene tradition are world-wide, for the Essene brotherhood was only one in a long series of mystical brotherhoods, linked by the same teaching and bearing the same mission. The 'Essene' tradition is even found among the Indian tribes of North and South America, the actual word 'Essene' is still revered by the Indians. Also the various clairvoyant visions and messages recorded in this book reveal how deeply it was a part of the hill-men of Britain. Their processional marches, their songs and music, their calling upon the angels—all these vouch for this. At Stone-henge they called down the four Angels; of the Sun, of the Waters; of the Air and of the Earth. With authority they claimed the angels' attendance, so they came. In this fashion all ancient peoples manifested their assurance of the goodness and care of Mother Earth for her children. The serpent-walks, also, with the projection of light up into the heavens above was again a claiming of man's sonship with his Heavenly

Father, and a working in conjunction with that Father to bless the earth with plenty.

Most of all did they affirm their belief in the Earthly Mother as demonstrated by the vision at Avebury, which had been so deeply impressed upon the ethers by the devotion of perhaps hundreds of generations of human souls.

XI

BRITAIN, ARISE!

DURING the damp and chilly July of 1968 we three—my wife, Jenny and myself—again visited Dragon Hill, this time travelling from Charney in Berkshire where we were staying for a few days. Despite the weather, Dragon Hill had in no way lost its magical power, as will be apparent from the scope and deeply mystical quality of the message received on this occasion, and which now follows.

DRAGON HILL, 15 JULY 1968

'I can see a vast gathering, but not of people of this earth. They are visitors from the etheric world. I can see these people perambulating the hillside, but what I am seeing all took place very long ago. Great angels surround us, the angels of the elements. Angels from the sun are descending from the heavens. I see a most wonderful light descending on Dragon Hill. Dragon Hill itself looks like a vast grail cup from which a beautiful gentle light is now rising. From these heights I can see the sun blazing, and framed in its light is the Christ figure, with arms outstretched pouring light like a blessing of love into the "grail cup." This "cup" represents the real heart of Britain. The watching and worshipping concourse reaches out and up towards the light. Indeed I see humanity as a whole race yearning for this spiritual illumination, and in response, the Christ figure (not Jesus) is reaching down, concentrating love and light on the earth. Again I see the brethren perambulating the hill, and at certain periods they turn inwards and raise their arms towards the light and towards this great symbolic figure.

'The dragon is a symbol of the struggle between the forces of light and darkness. Then this great Christ figure comes. The people are revived and strengthened by the light. All this represents a tremendous spiritual effort. There is fierce combat between the light and the dark forces. After a long battle the dragon is gradually overcome and slain. At last it lies dead.

'Then I see again what I have described before—the hill flooded with light. The vast "grail cup" is there again and the white essence it contains is poured out over the land.

'This battle I am seeing is symbolic of man's unending struggle upwards from the swamps, a raising-up of the people by the Christ Light.

'Evil is unevolved matter at its crude beginning. When the light permeates this matter it is gradually quickened and illumined until matter itself comes to life. The object of the process is to lighten and spiritualise all matter.

'A beautiful spiritual evolution has been taking place for age upon age as spirit has come deeper into matter—this gradual changing of darkness to light. When at last man responds to the light, he will no longer have to struggle for his existence, for his existence and freedom are there already in the light. He cannot help but be happy and healthy and create beauty as soon as he responds to the sun.

'At that same moment that man turns decisively away from his swamplands of materialism, a change will come in his etheric atoms and a spiritual light begin to irradiate him. He is a soul reborn.

'The story of the birth of Jesus in a stable, and of the coming of certain wise men from afar, is symbolic of the birth of the spiritual light, the Christ Light in man's heart, or in his "grail cup." This light in his heart is the source of all life, all that is good. It is the power which gives man his understanding of the eternal. Man cannot understand with his earthly mind what eternity means, but this light within him reveals the meaning to him. When he is raised in consciousness, when he is living in the light, then he will know.

'Do you remember how Moses came down out of the mountain bearing the stone tablets of the Law? The Law is written upon the stones—which means the very earth itself. It is in the very composition of the earth, in all nature, the trees, the flowers, the fruit, the grain, and creatures that move upon the earth. The Law is written in letters of light within matter itself! Let him look within, and man will find matter is light, and light is God, reflecting the very life of God.

'Something here feels most gentle, comforting and warm. . . . I can feel warmth all round me. I would say this was a particularly powerful centre of the grail ritual which goes far, far back, far beyond the Christian era to the very ancient brotherhood, and has been enacted again and again on the inner planes. Most beautiful rituals, beautiful ceremonies were enacted by these people in bygone days. These rituals will come back into use again, and become a great feature of life of man. When man understands, when he learns how to commune with etheric and angelic forces—as he will—he will discover that he has within himself the potentialities of God his Creator. He will learn how to create ideal form from the white ether. He will have power, knowledge and wisdom enough to use not only stone and brick, but the white ether itself with which to build his temples for the worship of his Creator.

'It looks to me as though Britain is as it were the central or "grail cup" of this whole planet. There are other beautiful centres in various parts of the world, but something uniquely pure and holy is here. It is this very purity and simplicity which is the saving grace of humanity.

'Britain must learn the meaning of the light and how to use the spiritual sunlight from the Solar Logos, the purity and holiness of which is man's salvation. This is the reason for the work and ritual of our Brotherhood of the White Eagle Lodge*—to project the rays of the pure light out to all people, as the brotherhoods have done from ancient times. Here in Britain is the point of balance of positive and negative forces between construction and destruction, which meet here. The forces of light will always triumph.'

White Eagle says:

'It is time for you all to understand the work which is now proceeding, the bringing into manifestation from the very soil of your island of the true light of spiritual brotherhood—brotherhood in very truth, not in word only but in life, in service, in kindness and co-operation, in patience, tolerance and love.

'This Brotherhood of the Great White Light is coming into full and glorious manifestation again. It will come through the real brotherhood of life. It will come into the hearts of tried and tested souls in groups of the White Brotherhood which will exist all over the world; but remember, the origin of this Brotherhood of the Great White Light is here, here in the mystic isle of Britain.

'The spirit of those great sun-gods, the god-men who first came to this ancient land of Britain, still lingers to inspire the people of this land to deeds of courage, kindness and goodwill. Be true to this ancient light. Be true to your great heritage, my brethren. Rise, put on your armour of light and work for

* See Appendix, p. 117.

the coming of the new day, not to satisfy any personal ambition or desire but for the coming of light and happiness and brotherhood to the land. Obey the urge towards service in every detail of your life.

'When as a nation you understand your great heritage, when you arise in the spirit of Christ, that is, in goodwill, justice, truth and brotherhood you will draw to yourselves all the nations. And although your land may not again be mighty in temporal power, it will once again become the centre of a great spiritual power for it is its destiny to rise again to become a spiritual leader of the world and to bring to fruition the ideal of universal brotherhood.

'Britain would at the present time appear to be in need of strength and help. Some pessimists may think that her power, her usefulness is fading. But this is not so. We tell you that within the soul of Britain is a light, a power, which will raise your country again to become a spiritual and moral leader of the whole world, not a country with great wealth and possessions, but a country free, ablaze with light.

'Follow the Star! Be true to the light within your hearts, to the light in Britain which is shining and which has shone in the hearts and lives of all those noble brothers, saints and teachers and servers of the past. Rise in spirit and fight the battle of spirit over darkness and despair, over the destruction of the lower mind and the ugliness which now prevails on the physical plane. Make your stand for truth, for beauty, for love and for the great brotherhood of all life.

'Let all your prayer and spiritual effort be dedicated to this end for even thus you will hasten the coming of Christ's kingdom upon earth.'

EPILOGUE

AGAIN we stand in fancy, you and I, on some height far above the prevailing earthiness; say, on a chalk down wide in expanse. Our feeling of height is due to its purity, to an abiding peace, to its wholesomeness and holiness. We stand beside a low earthen mound, once a burial-place for some sainted man or woman. His bones are now dust, but holy dust, impregnated with himself; and all the air around, and all the ethers, the flowers, the birds, the little creatures, they too know about the sainted one and in their way they worship.

Let us assume we stand on Maiden Castle, a wide expanse of downland guarded by banks and entrenchments, all erected since our saint's time, who knew none of these things. Neither did his people in the long ago. A thousand years, two, five thousand years—these are but insignificant periods of time which fleet past our sainted man like dream days; while as they fly, his essence remains because he and such as he are fathers to our Britain, and we are his sons who inherited his rich estate.

Somehow, we respond, we react. It comes to us as a wondrous feeling; so that we want to embrace, to hold the very soil close to ourselves.

The day is fine, warm and dry. Now we lie stretched at full length upon the short turf, trodden these many thousand years past by human feet; and as we lie the savour of it reaches down into us, deeply, full of rustlings and the runnings of tiny creatures. We bury our face in sweet grass; and then most wondrously, our heaviness of body departs. Our coat-of-skin thins away. We feel no longer boxed-down in flesh, but are lightened, illumined by a kind of luminous ether. We feel, we know that were we so inclined we could leap and run high and fast as never men have done before, that we are become light and ageless. Yet heaviness and ageing still wait like a bad dream in our background—this also we know, while feeling still above and beyond such heaviness.

Now have our senses also become finer, rarer; we are aware as never before of how close are the little people. They rustle and cluster around us now, prying, peeping, all-an-itch with curiosity. We do not take them too closely to ourselves, do not give out too much, lest we dissipate our nerve force, our soul force. Instead, we go deeper within.

Then we forget all else, even this Edenic land of which our souls have reached, in which we momentarily live. For now a power comes such as we have no words to describe, but can only feel as a glowing inflow of life. It seems to fill all earth and the skies above, reaching out to, pervading, quickening all things—indeed, hushing all troublous, clamouring thoughts until silence itself becomes quickened with its glory and wonder.

Then do we know but one truth only, one truth surely; that there be neither death nor evil ruling in this world of ours, that neither can endure. That all creation works towards life eternal, life enduring, everlasting. In this certitude we rest. In this surpassing surety we abide, all problems solved at last.

APPENDIX

CERTAIN points in the text call for further comment, which is incorporated in appendix form in order not to interrupt the narrative.

'On these hills an observatory was built. . .'

page 19, line 22

R. Hippisley Cox, in *The Green Roads of England* says: 'It is hardly accurate any longer to speak of them (the ancient men of Britain) as "Prehistoric," for the men who lie buried in the chambered barrows have left evidences of their lives, beliefs and doings almost as full as the written documents of a later day. . . . Settling in the land sometime between 10,000 B.C. and the date of the last glacial period, and the introduction of the Bronze about 2,000 B.C., they accomplished as much as modern men with similar limited means could do today. Their brain pans were as large as those of the modern European; they worshipped the sun, studied the heavens, believed in a life after death, and intellectually appear to have been superior to the race which succeeded them. They not only knew the use of fire and boiling water, domesticated their animals and grew grain, but from the evidences of their fortresses seem to have preserved peace and exercised a wide authority over the land.'

The Christ Spirit

page 21, lines 10 and 21

The reference is not to the man Jesus Christ of the Gospels but to the Cosmic Christ, third aspect of the Deity who can and does take human form as a spiritual being for our human understanding. The Christ spirit also dwells in the heart of every soul on earth—the creative impulse to good in man's being, and the activating force behind all the good in the world. This Christ light in man gradually grows in power through the experience of many, many incarnations until man himself becomes wholly irradiated. There have been many Christed ones throughout the ages, but for us today Jesus Christ is the supreme example of man made perfect—a Christed one.

Atlantis

page 24, line 23; page 77 line 10

White Eagle has often spoken of life on the lost continent of Atlantis. He has described the people as very highly civilised, but much more 'joyous and childlike' than people today. He speaks of these times as golden and sunlit until misuse of magical power brought about the final cataclysm which de-stroyed the continent. He says: 'From god-men, radiant beings not of earth evolution, the people of Atlantis received know-ledge of the Sun—not merely the physical or visible sun, but the only-begotten Son of the Father, Who is the Source of all life. They learnt that the rays of sunlight contained forces which could be harnessed for many purposes. They had know-ledge of motive power. We were accustomed to using air ships, and there were even quite small contrivances used by the individual to travel from place to place. Air ships, and stages for putting down and taking up passengers, usually on a hilltop or a hillside, were no uncommon sight, and this motive power was used in many ways for the convenience and well-being of the people.

'The sun's rays were also employed to give healing when necessary, as in the case of the young souls then coming into incarnation, for remember, two types were in incarnation at that time—those who were ready to be instructed in the magic of the White Light, and also those younger souls who were unready. In after ages the younger brethren became curious, and tried to discover the mysteries being revealed in the temples on the sacred mountains, thinking to gain power for themselves. They attained such power as the centuries passed, and eventually it came to them so rapidly that they, and finally the whole continent, without the spiritual development necessary to use such power wisely, were overwhelmed by catastrophe. The equilibrium of the whole earth was upset, and cataclysms and destruction followed. Many souls in incarnation today are facing karma made during that period.

'Not only were the neophytes instructed in the use of light and colour, but also they were initiated into the secrets of how to command the angelic forces, and thus control the air currents and the resultant weather. Agriculture thus became an exact science.

'One vivid memory remains with us of a time when instructions were received from the god-men, even then withdrawing from the earth plane, who said there was to be a great emigration, and that certain groups of brothers of the White Light, the white magic, were to journey afar. We have memories of ships setting forth and journeying northward to reach the west coast of what is now Great Britain, but which then formed a part of a greater island which was really the northern extremity of Atlantis.

'Centres of power still remain in Great Britain established by the White Brothers from Atlantis. At such centres the earth is impregnated with the magical rays behind the sunlight.

'The southern continent of America was visited, and we remember the holy mountain in the Andes, where another band of white brethren settled. The brothers wore white robes, ornamented with gold, colours associated always with the Brotherhood of the White Light. They also wore a crown of feathers earned in the course of severe training before initiation into the mysteries. Folk-tales and myths remain among the American Indians about the plumed men who brought light and salvation to them. The Indians also tell of the great flood, or the sinking of Atlantis.

'Some of the brethren journeyed to Egypt. The great pyramid is built on a similar plan and shape to the white temples in Atlantis. Pyramids still existing in America, in Egypt and in India are all relics of the buildings of the white brothers from Atlantis.

'We remember well those sacred times when the priests of the Sun, or of the White Light mysteries, gathered together with all the simple people of the villages to celebrate the special festivals. I remember the fire ceremonies at the solstices, ceremonies of welcome to the sun-spirits, and also the wonderful and powerful ceremony when we paced the path of the sun in two great wheels, the positive and negative, in a temple or lodge not confined by walls and roof, but open to the sky and stars. These ceremonies continued throughout night and day, and for many days.

'You have lost full knowledge of the power of the Sun, but this knowledge will return when the age of Brotherhood is fully established, but there must be true brotherhood of the spirit, and wisdom in men's hearts before the white magic of Atlantis can be fully regained for the blessing of mankind.'

The Hoerbiger Theory

page 52, line 12; page 77, line 14

References to a catastrophic impact with the earth from outer space recall to mind the work of Hans Hoerbiger whose *Cosmic Ice Theory* published in 1913 in collaboration with Philip Fauth, a German selenologist of high standing, aroused much controversy at the time. Hoerbiger suggests that our present moon is but one of a succession of moons which over vast periods of time have been 'caught' by our earth's attraction. According to him our moons were not broken off from the earth itself, as the current theory goes, but were fragments of one-time worlds circling in space which were caught up by the earth's attraction, and unable to escape, finally plunged in fragments into the earth. Indeed our present moon, some astronomers tell us, is also gradually yielding itself to the earth's attractive power, gradually edging nearer to the earth. In course of time, half a million or more years, say, she may suffer the fate of a former moon, the tertiary moon of Hoerbiger's theory.

We have to visualise this tertiary moon encircling our earth several million years ago perhaps, and then as ages pass gradually drawing closer and closer to the earth, growing ever bigger and brighter until its reflection of the sun outshines the sun itself. As it tears round the earth in twenty-four hours of perpetual 'daylight,' filling the whole expanse of the sky with itself, giant rainstorms begin, with quakes and tidal waves; and then the moon begins to disintegrate, scattering her pieces across the earth, so that great expanses of sea look as if afire, like a sheet of flame. At last the moon breaks up, her fragments burying themselves deeply into the earth. (It is suggested that this is why isolated pockets of minerals—often iron ore—

are found deeply embedded in various parts of the earth today.)

Following on the release of the vast bulge of waters of the equator, so the theory goes, tidal waves sped across the earth's surface, causing widespread inundation. For instance it is said that the whole Mediterranean area was once low-lying land, and that the ocean waters broke through at the Gibraltar gap and flooded all that land making it into sea.

If the earth were peopled at these times, many must have perished, and those who survived would have a searing memory left to hand on to their children, in stories of catastrophe on a world-wide scale—stories which have persisted as myths stamped on deep-seated racial memories of our peoples.

Hans Hoerbiger gained a disciple in an Englishman, H. S. Bellamy, who put the theory across to the English-speaking public in several books, notably *Moon*, *Myths and Man* (Faber & Faber) in which he seeks to corroborate the Hoerbiger theory by means of myth and folklore of all countries. He cites hundreds of myths which, if myths are fossilised history, as has been suggested, lend strong support to the theory. One has in mind Plato's story of Atlantis and also our own biblical story of the flood and the salvation of Noah's family. With these myths stand a host of others. In Mr. Bellamy's book he cites more than five hundred, told by two hundred and fifty differing peoples and tribes, some of them, notably the Red Indian and Maya accounts told with as much detail, and with even greater poetry and beauty than the Noah story.

Myth has it that after the flood men and women were guided into a bright land of the future, flowing with milk and honey, where they entered upon an age of purity and innocence. This age must also have dawned on our Britain.

Another vision on the part of my wife bears on this same

subject. We were staying on the ancient and holy isle of Iona in the Western Hebrides. We had climbed the island's only hill, Dun-I, from which the island of Staffa, with its magic Fingal's Cave, can be seen. To the east lies Mull, with Ben More standing guard over the island across the Sound. While sitting there, absorbing the peace and blessing of the place, my wife found herself in contact with one whom she took to be St. Columba, who revealed himself as one of the ancient brotherhood. Then her vision opened still further, to the far, far past.

'Now I see something very strange,' she said. 'I am told to look out across the seas and they are all on fire! The sky seems to be on fire too. This happened a very long time ago, how long ago I do not know, but it must really have happened, because it is recorded on the ether, or on the akasha. It is as if I were looking at a picture which is alive and moving, and all in colour. The sight is beautiful but frightening. I think I am contacting a time when a great upheaval took place. I think that some of the islands on the earth once formed part of other bodies, drawn by the force of gravity towards the earth.

'I am being shown that we are too limited by the idea of time in our conception of truth. We are too apt to think always in terms of hours, months and years. We regard 12,000 years ago as a great period of time, but in reality it is as nothing. Man has to realise that life was stirring in our solar system millions of years ago; but his earthly mind is so limited.

'To grasp the real nature of the life which now fills this earth planet we have ourselves to reach the state of consciousness which is outside time. At the beginning human beings who were great teachers came to earth; they had developed certain physical faculties and equipment to enable them to exist in a natural world while still retaining the mental and spiritual equipment of a heavenly order. They were visitors from outer space, drawn into the earth's atmosphere and life. They had power to envelop early humanity with solar rays and to infuse them with certain solar elements until such time as the spark of divine consciousness within the early man became quickened. We have no conception of time, or the divine life filling all things with itself, and which has always been in existence. This divine life, the centre of all things is God.

'We cannot get outside or beyond it, because we ourselves are part of God. This centre or God is all love, and we are within it.'

Evidence of Pre-Civilisations

The following extract from an article in *The Times* (26th June, 1971) 'Prehistoric Spacemen?' by Vera Brittain is reproduced from *The Times* by permission:

'In Ecuador platinum ornaments have been found which show the ancient Indians had furnaces which could heat to over a temperature of 1,770° centigrade although in Europe we have only been able to do this for two centuries. The Babylonian astronomers knew the crescent of Venus and the moons of Jupiter and Saturn, and the Dogon tribe in Africa knew about the star of Sirius though none of these are visible except through the most powerful of modern telescopes. Sanscrit texts estimated the life span of the universe in milliards of years as does modern science. In Peru, England and California, three iron nails have been found embedded in rock thousands of years older than iron. All these and many more scientific mysteries point to the existence of a prehistoric technology of which we know nothing today.

Andrew Tomas suggests in a book just published, *We are*

not the First, Souvenir Press, £2, that some of this scientific legacy was passed to the ancient civilisations we know a little about from still more ancient civilisations destroyed by tidal waves and the fires of submarine volcanoes in a geological upheaval.

The more startling hypothesis that such scientific knowledge may actually have been brought to earth from outer space is not new, but it gains credibility from Mr. Tomas's interpretation.

The American Astrophysicist Carl Sagan believes that visitations to earth from outer space take place at 500-year intervals. If history does stretch behind the 7,000 year limit afforded to it by the historians and if men lived in the last inter-glacial age perhaps an era of culture and advanced technology was started by the god-kings common in the legends of Mexico, Peru, Egypt, India, China and Greece.

. . . Such cosmic attempts to explain the inexplicable are not to everyone's taste, but Mr. Tomas's tracing of waves of knowledge back to an advanced race which is not recorded in history is a convincing answer to more mysteries like these; why the ancients knew about America, Antarctica and Iceland; why vaccination is described in the 3,500-year-old Vedas; why robots and computers appear in classic as well as medieval writings; why the Mayan calendar is so much more complex than our own. . . .

*The White Eagle Brotherhood and
White Eagle Lodge*

page 104, line 6

The reference is to the inner Brotherhood of the White Eagle Lodge, formed in 1934 under instruction from the Brotherhood beyond the veil, to work on the inner planes of life to help humanity through what were described as 'the years of fire'—that period of social upheaval, war and natural disaster which marks the transition from the Age of Pisces to the new Age of Aquarius. The brothers, dedicated to a life of service and self-discipline, have been taught how to use the power of God within their own souls in the cause of international peace and brotherhood and 'to heal, to comfort, to illumine' the souls of men—not so much by words or outward action, but silently, on the inner planes. Spiritual power is generated by certain rituals which we now know hark back to that far older Brotherhood which has existed through the ages. More about this ancient Brotherhood and the work of the Brotherhood today can be found in Grace Cooke's *The Illumined Ones*.

The White Eagle Lodge was founded in 1936 to practise and demonstrate White Eagle's teachings. It exists to help people to understand the reason for their life on earth and how to live in harmony with the whole brotherhood of life, visible and invisible, in health and happiness. Readers wishing to know more of the work of the White Eagle Lodge may write to the General Secretary, the White Eagle Lodge, New Lands, Rake, Liss, Hampshire; or can call at the White Eagle Lodge, 9 St. Mary Abbot's Place, London W.8.